EASEMENTS
AND
REVERSIONS

EASEMENTS
AND
REVERSIONS

by

Donald A. Wilson

Landmark Enterprises
10324 Newton Way
Rancho Cordova CA 95670

ISBN: 0-910845-43 -3

TABLE OF CONTENTS

Preface
Acknowledgement

Table of Contents (continued)

Table of Contents (continued)

Table of Contents (continued)

PREFACE

Over the years there have been many articles concerning easements and several books which either made easements their focus, or devoted a separate chapter to them. While the emphasis has been on what an easement is, and how easements are created, little analysis has appeared on the termination of easements and the fate of the land burdened by them.

This treatment attempts to address that topic and the reversion rights and boundaries that accompany easement termination. Reversions are constant problems for surveyors and title examiners, so it is anticipated that this will serve as a guide useful in the solution of those problems.

ACKNOWLEDGEMENT

I wish to express my appreciation to those persons who as-
sisted with the publication of this book. My wife, Christine,
proofread the manuscript and made many helpful suggestions, both editorial and in terms of content. Bob Cox, LLS,
helped me in much the same way by making numerous suggestions and offering guidance in the way certain concepts
were presented. David Connell, Attorney, gave me a critical
review from a legal standpoint. His suggestions in the form
of concepts and recent significant court decisions help to
round out the text material.

Two other attorneys should be acknowledged as well. My
friends, Fran Lane and Scott La Pointe both offered encour-
agement and reinforcement of the need for such work. To
them I offer thanks.

Finally, to Roy Minnick, my editor and publisher, I am
deeply appreciative of the support and willingness to offer
suggestions and guidance in doing this type of publication.
His uncanny way of making a writer's job easier and his en-
couragement in keeping me continually moving forward sig-
nificantly helped to make this book a reality.

1. EASEMENTS IN GENERAL

DEFINITION. An *easement* has been defined as "a right, privilege, or liberty which one has in land owned by another; it is a right to a limited use in another's land for some special and definite purpose.[1] It is important to understand every facet of that definition since it not only states what an easement is, but also limits its scope.

First, an easement is *a right, privilege, or liberty;* it is not ownership of the fee, or of the land itself. It is called a non-possessory interest in land since the owner of the easement does not possess the land itself — he merely has the right to do certain acts in the land of another. However, it is more than a mere personal privilege, it constitutes an *actual interest in the land* and thus is regarded as realty.[2]

Secondly, an easement is *in land of another,* therefore one cannot have

---

[1] Maine Real Estate Law, Chapter 6.
Mass. App. 1980. "Easement" is a right which one person has to use the land of another for a definite purpose. Brown v. Sneider, 400 N. E. 2d 1322, 9 Mass. App. 329.

[2] Maine Real Estate Law, Chapter 6.
N.Y.A.D.2 Dept. 1984. "Easement" is interest in land created by grant or agreement, express or implied, which confers right upon holder thereof to some profit, benefit, dominion, enjoyment or lawful use out of or over estate of another; thus, holder of easement falls within scope of generic term "owner." Copertino v. Ward, 473 N.Y.S.2d 494, 100 A.D.2d 565.

an easement on one's own land.³   This becomes a critical point when *merger of title* takes place. More will be said about merger of title in the chapter on termination of easements.

Last, an easement is a *right to a limited use . . . . for some special and definite purpose*. Therefore an easement holder may not do anything and everything on the land or a portion thereof as if he had full ownership of it. He may only do certain things, whatever is specified in the grant or travels with the easement, and only for a special and definite purpose, not whatever he wishes to do.⁴

An easement is also often defined as being a right which one has in land of another *not inconsistent*   with a general property in the owner.⁵ However, this is not always the case as easements created many years ago may still be in effect and be contrary to the present owner's plans for use of the land, or even may prevent certain uses. Many of these outstanding easements may be very burdensome in that they are superior rights having been conveyed away years ago.⁶ If created, or conveyed, very long ago they may

---

³ 25 Am. Jur. 2d § 2. A person cannot have an easement in his own land, since all the uses of an easement are fully comprehended in his general right of ownership.

The reason why one may not have an easement in his own land is that an easement merges with the title, and while both are under the same ownership the easement does not constitute a separate estate. Sievers v. Flynn, 305 Ky 325, 204 SW2d 364.

One cannot be said to have an easement in lands the fee simple to which is in himself. Othen v. Rosier, 148 Tex 485, 226 SW2d 622.

Mass. 1863. While two adjoining estates are both owned by the same person, no easement can be created in one of them for the benefit of the other. Carbey v. Willis, 89 Mass. 364, 83 Am. Dec. 688.

⁴ 25 Am. Jur. 2d, § 72. A principle which underlies the use of all easements is that the owner of the easement cannot materially increase the burden of the servient estate or impose thereon a new and additional burden. Though the rights of the easement are paramount, to the extent of the easement, to those of the landowner, the rights of the easement owner and of the landowner are not absolute, irrelative, and uncontrolled, but are so limited, each by the other, that there may be a due and reasonable enjoyment of both the easement and the servient tenement. The owner of an easement is said to have all rights incident and necessary to its proper enjoyment, but nothing more.

⁵25 Am. Jur. 2d, § 1.

⁶ Grantees take title to land subject to duly recorded easement which have been granted by their predecessors in title. Borders v. Yarborough, 75 S.E.2d 541, 237 N.C. 540; Waldron v. Town of Brevard, 62 S.E.2d. 512, 233 N.C. 26.

be outside of the realm of a normal title examination and not be discovered under present title examination standards. Even though a matter of record, an easement may only appear outside of the period of search.

SYNONYMOUS WITH SERVITUDE. A *servitude* is the term used in the civil law to express the idea conveyed by the word *easement* in the common law, and may be defined as a right of the owner of one parcel of land, by reason of his ownership, to use the land of another for a special purpose of his own, not inconsistent with the general property of the owner.[7] Servitude should not, however, be construed as the same as equitable servitude, which is a form of restrictive covenant.

DISTINGUISHED FROM LICENSE. An easement is distinguished from a *license* by the latter being a mere *revocable* right, privilege or permission to enter upon or do acts upon another's land.[8] A license is usually very temporary, generally may not be either bought or sold and is revocable at any time, or in some cases may be permanent, and treated in much the same as fee ownership.

Examples of licenses would be the right to leave your car in a parking area when visiting the movies, or having verbal or written permission to walk on a neighbor's land when doing a survey.

DISTINGUISHED FROM PROFIT. A *profit a prendre*, also called "right of common", is a right exercised by one person in the soil of another, accompanied with participation in the profits of the soil. It is not an easement since one of the features of an easement is the absence of right to participate in the profits of the soil charged with it. It is similar to an easement, however, in that it is an interest in the land. It is created by grant, and may be either appurtenant or in gross.[9]

Examples of rights of *profit a prendre* are the right to cut timber, the right to take gravel,[10] soil, coal or minerals generally from the land of anoth-

---

[7] 25 Am. Jur. 2d, § 1.

[8] Maine Real Estate Law, Chapter 6.

[9] 25 Am. Jur. 2d, § 4.

[10] The words "reserving the gravel" in a deed created in the grantor a profit a prendre. Beckwith v. Rossi, 157 Me. 532, 174 A2d 732.

er, the right to graze animals and the rights to fish or hunt. Flowing water is not considered a product of the soil therefore the right to take such is an easement, not a *profit a prendre.* A right to take ice,[11] however, has sometimes been considered as a right of *profit a prendre.*[12]

RESTRICTIVE COVENANTS. Restrictive covenants as to the use of the land or the location and character of improvements have been said to create easements. Such covenants, being limitations on the manner in which one may use his land, do not create true easements, but only rights in the nature of servitudes or easements, sometimes characterized as "negative easements" or "reciprocal negative easements."[13]

NATURAL RIGHTS. Certain rights, such as lateral and subjacent support of the land in its natural condition, or the right to receive the benefit of the flow of a natural watercourse and the discharge of surface water from a higher to lower plane, are said to be inherent in the land, and are termed "natural rights." They have been said to have similarity to easements, but they are not true easements, since they have not been created by an act of man.[14]

TERMINOLOGY OF EASEMENTS. The land benefited by an easement is known as the *dominant tenement,* while the land burdened by the easement is known as the *servient tenement.*[15]

---

[11] The grant of a right to harvest ice amounts to more than merely a revocable license, it constitutes a right in the nature of an easement appurtenant to the land or a profit a prendre. Gadow v. Hunholz, 160 Wis. 293, 151 NW 810.

[12] 25 Am. Jur. 2d, § 4.

[13] 25 Am. Jur. 2d, § 5.

[14] 25 Am. Jur. 2d, § 6.

[15] Maine Real Estate Law, Chapter 6.

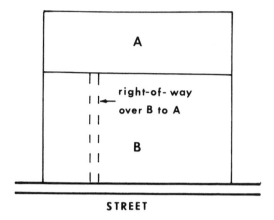

Figure 1.1   The owner of A, being benefited by the right-of-way, is the dominant tenement, *while B, being burdened by the right-of-way, is the* servient tenement.

EASEMENTS APPURTENANT AND IN GROSS. Easements may be categorized into appurtenant, or in gross. If the easement was created for the purpose of benefiting *other land* owned by the holder of the easement, it is *appurtenant* — that is, appurtenant to the land it benefits.[16]

Appurtenant easements *run with the land* and are a part of a conveyance of land, whether mentioned in the conveyance or not.[17]   The saying goes, "once an easement, always an easement," is true, and easements do not automatically "go away" if they are not described in a conveyance, or if they

---

[16] Maine Real Estate Law, Chapter 6; Davis v. Briggs, 117 Me. 536, 105 A. 128 (1918).

[17] R.I. 1924. A deed which conveyed the dominant estate passed an easement which ran with the land, though the deed did not mention such easement. Khouri v. Dappinian, 125 A. 268, 46 R.I.163.

When an easement, though not originally belonging to land, has become appurtenant to it by grant or prescription, a conveyance of the land will carry with it such easement, whether mentioned in the deed or not, though it may not be necessary to the enjoyment of the land by the grantee. Me. 1894. Cole v. Bradbury, 29 A. 1097, 86 Me. 38; Me. 1866. Dority v. Dunning, 6 A. 6, 78 Me. 381.

are not used.[18]   Extinguishment, or termination, of easements will be examined in detail as subject matter of Chapter 4.

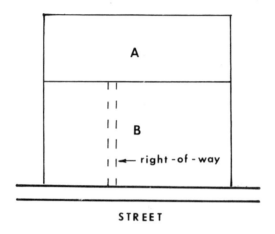

*Figure 1.2   The right-of-way over Lot B to benefit Lot A is appurtenant
to Lot A.*

A easement *in gross* does not benefit any other land; it exists independently of other land, and is a mere personal interest in or right to use the land of another.[19]   In other words, there is a servient tenement but no domi-

---

[18] As a general rule, an easement acquired by grant or reservation cannot be lost by mere nonuser for any length of time, no matter how great. 23 Am. Jur. 2d, § 105.

[19] Maine Real Estate Law, Chapter 6.

An easement in gross cannot be acquired except by grant or by prescription. Branan v. Wimsatt, 298 F. 833, 54 App. D.C. 374 certiorari denied 44 S.Ct. 639, 265 U.S. 591, 68 L. Ed. 1195; Miller v. Lutheran Conference & Camp Ann'n. 200 A. 646, 331 Pa. 241, 130 A.L.R. 1245.

The general rule in the United States today with respect to easements in gross is that if they are commercial in character, such as railroad or public utility easements, they are transferable, non-commercial easements in gross are transferable only if such intention is indicated in its creation, such as by the use of the words "heirs and assigns.": 2 Am. L. Prop. § 8.75; RESTATEMENT § 489, 491.

nant tenement.[20]   Examples of easements in gross are utility rights-of-way and the right to flow land with water around a stream or pond which is being dammed.

DETERMINATION WHETHER EASEMENT IS APPURTENANT OR IN GROSS. Whether a particular easement is classed as appurtenant or in gross, and sometimes it is difficult to tell which it is, depends mainly on its nature and the intention of the parties creating it.[21]   If the easement is in its nature an appropriate and useful adjunct of the land conveyed, having in mind the intention of the parties as to its use and there is nothing to show that the parties intended it to be a more personal right, it should be held to be an easement appurtenant and not an easement in gross.[22]   Easements in gross are not favored by the courts, however, and an easement will never be presumed as personal when it may fairly be construed as appurtenant to some other estate. If doubt exists as to its real nature, an easement is presumed to be appurtenant, and not in gross.[23]

---

[20] For example, a public utility company's easement to place and maintain power lines across another's land. Maine Real Estate Law, Chapter 6.

Easement in gross usually has no dominant estate; it is purely servient. DeShon v. Parker, 361 N.E.2d 457, 3 O.O.3d 430.

[21] There is no incompatibility in the grant of a right of way to several persons, which grant confers a right appurtenant as to some of the grantees and a right in gross as to the others; such a grant may be partly appurtenant and partly in gross. Louisville & N.R. Co. v. Koelle, 104 111. 455. Davis v. Briggs, 105. 117. Me. 536.

Me. 1918. An "easement in gross" because of its personal nature is not assignable or inheritable, but an "easement appurtenant" runs with the land. Davis v. Briggs, 205 A.128, 117 Me. 536.

Vt. 1950. In determining whether there was an easement in gross or an appurtenant easement, intent of parties to be gathered from the nature of the subject matter and language used in deed, was required to control. A construction that an easement is one appurtenant rather than in gross is favored. Sabins v. McAllister, 76 A.2d 106, 116 Vt. 302.

[22] Greenwalt v. McCardell, 178 Md 132, 12 A.2d 522; Smith v. Dennedy, 224 Mich 378, 194 NW 998; American Rieter Co. v. Dinallo, 147 A.2d 290.

[23] 25 Am. Jur. 2d, § 13.

R.I. 1927. In case of doubt presumption favors easement being appurtenant. Sullivan Granite Co. v. Vuono, 137 A. 687, 48 R.I. 292.

Whether an easement is appurtenant or in gross is to be determined by a fair interpretation of the grant or reservation creating the easement, aided, if necessary, by the situation of the property and the surrounding circumstances.[24]

AFFIRMATIVE OR NEGATIVE. Easements may also be classed as either *affirmative* or *negative.* An affirmative easement is one which *allows* the holder of the easement to do certain acts on land of another.[25]

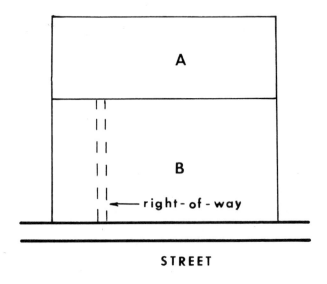

Figure 1.3   A right-of-way over Lot B to access Lot A is an affirmative easement in favor of the owner of Lot A.

---

[24] 25 Am Jur. 2d, § 13.

[25] Maine Real Estate Law, Chapter 6

A negative easement is one which allows the holder of the easement to *prevent* an owner from doing certain acts on his *own* land.[26]

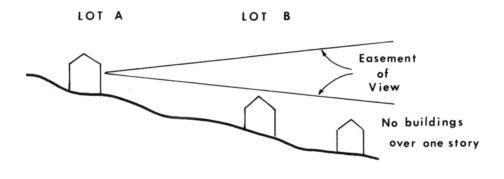

Figure 1.4   An easement of view owner by owner A is a negative easement over Lot B preventing him from interfering with A's view.

Another example of a negative easement is a conservation easement, by which the development rights of the parcel are permanently controlled.

APPARENT OR NONAPPARENT. Easements have been classed as apparent or nonapparent. An *apparent easement*, as the name implies, is one which is obvious, and one which is understood to be open and visible, such as a pathway or road. The word "apparent", however does not necessarily mean actual visibility, but rather "susceptibility of ascertainment on reasonable inspection by persons ordinarily conversant with the subject." An underground drain may be an apparent easement, although not visible from the

---

[26] Maine Real Estate Law, Chapter 6

surface.[27]

CONTINUOUS OR NONCONTINUOUS. Easements may also be continuous or noncontinuous. A continuous easement is one in which the enjoyment is, or may be, continuous without the necessity of any actual interference by man,[28] or as one depending on the natural formation of or some artificial structure upon, the servient tenement, obvious and permanent, such as the bed of a running stream, an over-hanging roof, a pipe for conveying water, a waterspout which discharges the water whenever it rains, a drain or a sewer.[29]

A noncontinuous easement is one which can only be enjoyed through the interference of man, that is, one which has no means specially constructed or appropriated to its enjoyment and which is enjoyed at intervals, leaving between those intervals no visible sign of its existence, such as a right of way or a right to draw water.[30]

---

[27] 25 Am Jur. 2d, § 9.

MD. 1947. An easement is "apparent" if its existence is indicated by signs which must necessarily be seen or which may be seen or known on careful inspection by persons ordinarily conversant with the subject. Slear v. Jankiewicz, 54 A.2d 137, 189 Md. 18, certiorari denied 68 S.Ct. 453, 333 U.S. 827, 92 L.Ed. 1112.

N.J. 1956. Where licensed surveyor, whom landowner had retained to survey tract for, inter alia, visible evidences of interests not appearing of record, did not discover such use of right of way by trucks going to and from loading platform on adjoining property as to warrant notice, such use of way for that purpose lacked those qualities of apparency and permanency essential to creation of easement by implied grant. A.J. and J.O. Pilar, Inc. v. Lister Corp., 123 A. 2d 536, 22 N.J. 75.

[28] The test of continuousness is that there is an alteration or arrangement, permanent in nature, which makes one tenement dependent in some measure on another. German Sav. & L. Soc. v. Gordon, 54 Or 147, 102 P. 736.

[29] 25 Am Jur. 2d, § 10.

[30] Ibid

A way is said to be a noncontinuous easement, because in the use of it there is involved the personal action of the owner in walking or driving on it. Hoffman v. Shoemaker, 69 W. Va. 233, 71 SE 198.

A cement driveway between houses on adjoining lots, though a visible easement, is not a continuous one. Milewski v. Wolski, 314 Mich. 445, 22 NW 2d 831, 164 ALR 998.

2.   KINDS OF EASEMENTS

There are nearly an infinite number of types of easements, as an easement, or right in another's land, may be created for almost any purpose. There are several kinds however, that are very commonplace and appear frequently in public records.

RIGHT OF WAY. Perhaps the most common of all easements, and the one which comes readily to mind when the word "easement" is used, is a right-of-way Rights-of-way may be in any one of a number of different forms, however, such as a right-of-way for ingress and egress, a power line or other utility line, a pipeline or a highway.

A right of way is the privilege which one person or class of people have of passing over the land of another in some particular line. It is an easement, but the term is used to describe either the easement itself or the strip of land which is occupied for the easement.[1]

A right of way may be public or private, and public ways as applied to ways by land are usually termed "highways" or "public roads," and every citizen has the right to their use. A private way, to the contrary, relates to that class of easements in which a particular person or particular description or class of people has an interest or right, as distinguished from the general public. Generally, a private way is a way for travel over the surface of land, but there may also be a right of way over a passageway or stairway.[2]

[1] 25 Am. Jur. 2d § 7
[2] Ibid.

EXAMPLE:

> "... with liberty to pass into said garret by the front stairs, & also liberty
> to use the front entry & front door, together with the privilege of passing & be-
> tween the road house as much as is necessary. .."

*Copy from an 1803 document giving several rights in the premises, in-
cluding the right to use the front stairs.*

The word "alley" when used in a deed between individuals, frequently
means a "private way."[3]

Rights of way for ingress and egress, or to pass over a person's land,
may not be obvious. They may not be readily visible on the surface of the
earth, and even though on the public record, may be well outside the period
of time examined in a normal title search.[4]   Those not mentioned in title

---

[3] Ibid.

[4] In searching titles for the existence of way it is necessary to search both the dominant and servient tenement. Usually the servient tenement makes no mention of being
burdened by the easement. An owner of the servient tenement conveyed the easement to
an owner of the dominant tenement at some point in time. It is necessary to identify that
conveyance and that point in time as it may never be mentioned in any of the conveyances of the dominant tenement. A common example of that is when the easement is
created in a will, or more often, in a partition of the real estate among heirs. Frequently
subsequent deeds to the various parcels do not mention the easement(s), but the right(s)
exists and "runs with the land" until its termination.

documents, but created in other ways are particularly troublesome, as dependence is often on evidence of use or parol testimony. These would never appear in a title examination but might be shown on a survey of the premises. A researcher should be on the alert for such evidence as it indicates an encumbrance on the land.

The highway right-of-way, or easement, is the most frequent type subject to the process of *reversion*. Chapter 6 will be devoted to this important subject.

RIGHT OF WAY LINE. A common misunderstanding is in the use of the term *right of way*. As stated previously, the term may be used to describe both the easement itself or the strip of land which is occupied for the easement.[5]

The *right of way line* is the line at the edge of the easement, defining its extent. Generally there are two, one on either side. Often the term right of way is used when the land itself is not an easement, but a strip owned in fee by another. A common example of this is a railroad "right-of-way." Most railroad beds are owned in fee by the railroad company. A few are easements, and occasionally one is based on a lease.

---

[5] The term"right-of-way" has a two fold signification. It sometimes is used to describe a right belonging to a party — a right of passage over any tract; and it is also used to describe that strip of land which railroad companies take upon which to construct their roadbed. Maysville & B.S.R. Co. v. Ball, 56 S.W. 188, 108 Ky 241.

Term "right of way" in deed is frequently used to describe not only easement but the strip of land occupied by such use. Moakley v. Los Angeles Pac. Ry. Co., 34 P.2d 218, 139 Cal. App. 421.

A "right of way" may consist of either of the fee or merely of a right of passage and use or servitude. Brightwell v. International - Great Northern R. Co. (Tex.) 41 S.W.2d 319.

In railroad parlance, "right of way" means either strip of land on which track is laid or legal right to use such land, and in latter sense may mean easement. Quinn v. Pere Marquette Ry. Co., 239 N.W. 376, 256 Mich. 143.

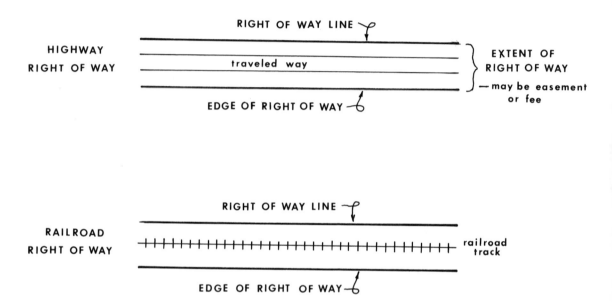

Figure 2.1 Examples of right of way - highway and railroad.

The following description is from a deed conveying the fee to a 20-foot strip to be used as a right-of-way to the lake:

EXAMPLE:

"Also a certain piece or parcel of land shown on said plan as a 20-foot passway located between said Wentworth Cove Road and Lake Winnipesaukee and situated southerly of Lot #1 as shown on said plan and between said Lot #1 and an unnumbered lot owned by one O'Callaghan."

FLOWAGE EASEMENTS. A flowage easement is the right a person, or group of persons, has to flood water on land of another, or others.[6] Flowage easements are common, and can be very troublesome as many of them are very old, having been created many years ago. Especially troublesome are those based on mill rights or mill privileges, some of which were created in the 18th Century, even in the 17th Century, and are still rights outstanding and owned by another, although perhaps not utilized for a century or even longer. Flowage may be for the purpose of storing water for mill purposes, hydroelectric power, flood control or irrigation.

Another troublesome problem with flowage easements is that they were frequently granted for huge tracts, extending far inland from the lake or river. Some of these tracts have subsequently been subdivided without technically being released from the easements.

EXAMPLES:

"Reserving to the Salisbury Manufacturing Company the right to flow so much of said premises as may be by a dam seven and one-half (7 1/2) feet high at Trickling Falls and also reserving highway that passes over said land."

"Also a certain tract of land situated in Kingston, described as follows: Lying at the Northerly side leading from the New Boston Road so-called to Trickling Falls, and bounded: South by said road; West by S. S. Crafts land; North by Amos Currier's land, and East by Samuel L. Blaisdell's land. Containing twenty-two acres, more or less. Said land is sold subject to the right to flow the low land by the Amesbury and Salisbury Mfg. Co."

---

[6] Conn. 1959. Right of flowage is an easement. Gager v. Carlson, 150 A.2d 302, 146 Conn. 288.

Conn. 1940. The right of flowage is only an "easement."   Great Hill Lake v. Caswell, 11 A.2d 396, 126 Conn. 364.

The following description is a flowage easement over a 4-acre parcel:

"The full and free right to flow at all times by means of a dam to kept up and maintained at Trickling Falls in East Kington near the house of the late Jacob Gale at the full height of seven and one half feet measuring from the flow‐ing of the waterway as it now is, one undivided half part of the following de‐scribed piece of land owned jointly with Thomas Gould and bounded Easterly on Powow River, Southerly on land of Thomas Gould Westerly on land of William Webster and northerly on land of Thomas Gould, containing four acres be the same more or less."

A recent example of outstanding flowage rights was the case in Dover, New Hampshire where an individual purchased the rights from the State of New Hampshire to operate a long-abandoned hydroelectric power dam. In the process, the State did a normal title search for 35 years, which is the standard for marketability of title. But the purchaser, desirous to know the extent of his rights with his purchase, searched the records for a period of 135 years. As a result, he found that he had the right to erect flashboards on the dam and raise the level of the water an additional four feet. Being in the hydropower business, this was important to him, since it would enable him to produce considerably more power.[7] However, it was not without its consequences. Raising the water level an additional four feet would result in putting a City road entirely under water, flood acres of farmland and put several new and expensive homes in danger.[8]

Normal title examinations usually do not discover these easements unless they are carried forward in recent conveyances. Since title examination standards are merely standards defining the minimum examination that must be undertaken, frequently further search and investigation should be considered to identify such outstanding rights so they don't become a conflicting use of the land at sometime in the future. The more that hydropower is developed, the more important these outstanding rights will be.

PRIVATE USE OF WATER. A common right in the form of an easement in another's land, particularly an adjoiner, is that connected with the use of, or access to, water. Mostly this is for domestic purposes, but there are a number of examples of using water on another's land for watering animals, or using water from another's land for irrigation. Typical domestic uses are well rights, with access, rights to use a spring on nearby premises, and the right to lay and maintain pipes to draw water from a nearby source.

EXAMPLES:

> "Together with the right to draw water from a well located at the rear of the premises herein conveyed."

> "Reserving and excepting, however, the right to lay, maintain and repair a water pipe from said spring across the premises herein granted, for the purpose supplying water to other property of the said Herbert A. Manning on the other side of Summit Avenue. It is understood and agreed that the said George L. and Ruth E. Cutting do not undertake to assure the said Manning the right to use a part of the water supply from said spring, or to run a pipe from said spring to the premises herein granted; this reservation extending only

---

[7] The output would have increased from 900,000 KW-hours to about 1.2 million KW-hours.

[8] New York Times, 1985.

to the sharing of the water from said spring and the right to run a pipe across the premises herein granted."

"This conveyance is subject to, and includes all rights, if any, in the water supply for the described premises situated on property."

With the further right to lay, maintain and repair any and all pipes necessary over the grantor's premises to Lake Winnipesaukee at such location as may be agree upon for the purpose of furnishing the grantee's premises with Lake water.

DRAINAGE. Easements for drainage are very commonplace in recent subdivisions and along highways. Runoff has to be dealt with, and frequently drainage from streets is routed across subdivision lots and onto adjacent land. Without the right, the runoff could be considered a trespass, and could result in damages to land of another.

EXAMPLE:

This conveyance is also made subject to whatever rights of drainage and flowage, if any, the Winnipisseogee Lake Cotton & Woolen Manufacturing Co., or any others may have.

AERIAL. Easements through space for bridges and walkways between buildings are examples of aerial easements. They are three-dimensional in nature, having a planimetric description and elevations which control the vertical limits as a complementary description.

AVIGATION. Also three-dimensional are avigation easements, or the rights of airplanes to utilize the airspace over land parcels in their flight path in their approach to or takeoff from a runway. This is known as the *glide path*. Ordinarily, such an easement would be variable in the third dimension, being at 0 elevation closest to the end of the runway and becoming greater in height as one proceeds away from the runway.

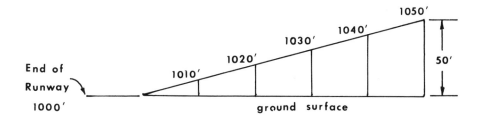

*Figure 2.2 Three dimensional easement for use of airspace
at end of runway.*

LIGHT AND AIR.[9]   Airspace, or air rights, includes so much of the
space above the ground as can be occupied or made use of, in connection
with enjoyment of the land. The right is not fixed, or constant, and varies
with varying needs and is coextensive with them. The owner of land owns
as much of the space above him as he uses, but only so long as he uses it.
Everything which lies beyond belongs to the world.[10]

Airplanes have a right to use airspace but since an owner of a tract of
land has unlimited air rights, he may convey his interest above the surface
or above a specified elevation. Condominium ownership consists of a spe-
cialized type of airspace ownership, having upper and lower horizontal limits.

[9] Mass. 1931. Easement of light and air is acquired only by express grant, by
covenant, or by implication. Novello v. Caprigno, 176 N.E. 809, 276 Mass. 34.

[10] Hand & Smith, Chapter 5. United States v. Causby, 328 U.S. 256 (1946).

The doctrine of ancient lights, recognized by English common law, protects a landowner's access to sunlight across neighboring property. When a dwelling has received sunlight across adjoining land for a specific period of time, the right to continue to enjoy such sunlight becomes part of the fee simple ownership of the property. Under the doctrine of ancient lights, the owner acquires a negative easement under the principle of prescription. Since 1832 the prescriptive period has been 20 years.[11] Some courts however, have decided to the contrary.[12]

SOLAR ENERGY. Because of its importance for energy, solar access is a right which has received attention in recent years. Recent court decisions have held that if sunlight is being utilized *for energy* adjoining landowners may not interfere with that use.[13]   Easements protecting neighboring airspace for access to sunlight will most certainly become more common.

OBSTRUCTION OF VIEW. Scenic view may enhance the value of a tract of land. In order to preserve and protect a view, an easement may well be in order.

---

[11] Hand & Smith, Chapter 5.

Prescription Act 1832, § 3

See also R.I. 1900. An easement in light cannot be acquired by prescription, but only by covenant or grant. Mathewson St. M.E. Church v. Shepard, 46 A. 402, 22 R.I. 112.

R.I. 1950. Landowner has no right to light and air coming to him across neighbor's land. Musumeci v. Leonardo, 75 A.2d 175, 77 R.I. 255.

Mass. 1870. It is well settled that by the common law a deed of land passes no right of light and air over other lands without express words. Brooks v. Reynolds, 106 Mass. 31.

[12] Mass. 1860. No prescriptive right to use of light and air through windows can be acquired by use and enjoyment. Richardson v. Pond, 81 Mass. 387; Keats v. Hugo, 115 Mass. 212.

Mass. 1921. Easement of light and air can exist only by express grant, covenant, or absolute necessity, and cannot be created by prescription. Tidd v. Fifty Associates, 131 N.E. 77, 238 Mass. 421.

S.C. 1936. Easements of unobstructed ocean view, breezes, light, or air do not exist. Schroeder v. O'Neill, 184 S.E. 679, 179 S.C. 310.

[13] Prah v. Maretti, 108 Wis. 2d 223, 321 NW2d 182 (1982) is the leading case. See also Tenn v. 889 Associates, 127 NH 321, 500 A.2d 366 (1985).

EXAMPLE:

"The grantors include a servitude in favor of the grantees over other land owned by the grantors and lying Southeastly of the granted premises so as to restrict to one and one-half stories the size of structures which may be erected Southerly of the line of sight from the Northeasterly corner of the granted premises to the Southeasterly corner of the remaining premises of the grantors at the Junction of the Lamprey River and land of Gallant."

MISCELLANEOUS USES OF EASEMENTS. As previously recognized, there are almost an infinite number of examples of, or uses for, easements. Grazing, utilities, protection from water and particularly, slopes for highways, are very common.

EXAMPLES:

Parcel #55, 56, 57 - General Utility Easement:

"Also taking the right and easement to construct and maintain utilities of any nature and kind, in upon, and over three certain parcels of land, in the Town of Salem, said parcels being described as follows:

Being all that land belonging to Donald Baron and Raymond N. Baron that lies between the taking described above and a line forty-four (44') feet westerly of and parallel with N. H. Route 28 Construction Base Line, said easement being on land which is bounded on the North by the Westerly Sideline of N. H. Route 28, as now traveled; bounded on the South by Town of Salem Right-of-Way; bounded on the East by the proposed Westerly Sideline of N.H. Route 28; and, bounded on the West by other land of Donald Baron and Raymond N. Baron, all in accordance with the above-referenced plan.

Containing three hundred ninety-two (392) square feet, more or less.

Parcel #55 - Channel Easement:

Also taking the permanent right and easement to improve the channel of the Spicket River, as shown on the above referenced plan.

Containing two hundred fifty (250) square feet, more or less.

Temporary Slope Easement:

Also taking the right and easement for the purpose of regrading, as necessary, in order to blend or match the remaining land with the new highway, all in accordance with the above-referenced plan. Ground so disturbed to be returned as near as possible to its original condition. Said easement to expire on December 31, 1989 by operation of this instrument.

Containing eight hundred sixty-five (865) square feet, more or less."

Some are unusual, but must be recognized and honored, as they are rights which either attach to land (appurtenant) or are for benefit or others independent of land (in gross), or burden land as a superior right conveyed away and owned by another, or others.

EXAMPLES:

"Also a privilege to dry clothes in said yard and to use the necessary in said yard in common with others and to pass and repass in the usual path from said brick building to said necessary."

"...reserve the right to pick blueberries on the granted premises so long as they do not interfere with the operations of the grantee."

"This deed is subject to a fifty (50) foot access easement and a beaver dam easement as shown on said plan."[14]

---

[14] In this particular case the easement was for the purpose of getting to a beaver dam located on the land of another, and being able to control the height of the dam to avoid excess flooding on the adjoining land.

3. CREATION OF EASEMENTS

There are eight ways by which an easement may be created:[1]

1.   Express grant
2.   Reservation or exception
3.   Agreement or covenant
4.   Implication
5.   Estoppel
6.   Prescription
7.   Dedication
8.   Eminent Domain

Easements may be classified as express, implied or prescriptive.[2] An express easement is created if the intent of the parties has been specifically evidenced by language in declaration or documents.[3]

Courts are also willing to recognize an easement without evidence of express intent if certain requirements are satisfied by the circumstances and conditions of affected properties.[4] Implied easements may be created

---

[1] Mass. 1830. Different persons may have a right of way over the same place by different titles, one by grant, another by prescription, and a third by custom. Kent v. White, 27 Mass. 138.

[2] Mass. 1912. An easement of a right of way can be created only by grant, express or implied, or by prescription, or by exception. Childs v. Boston & M.R.R., 99 NE 957, 213 Mass. 91, 48 LRA, NS 378.

[3] A Practical Guide to Disputes Adjoining Landowners - Easements § 1.01(2f).

[4] A Practical Guide to Disputes Adjoining Landowners - Easements § 1.01(2f).

due to compelling circumstances and prescriptive easements may be created through long-term use without permission or authorization.

BY EXPRESS GRANT. Usually called a "deeded easement," an easement may be created by *express grant*. It may be created by a deed or related instrument, but also may be created in a probate document.

By far the most commonly used method of creating an easement is by deed. The deed must describe the interest correctly and must comply with the formalities necessary for the transfer of any interest in land.[5] The conveyance should include words of inheritance and a statement of duration of the easement.

EXAMPLE:

"The Town of Kingston, a New Hampshire Municipal Corporation, located in the County of Rockingham and State of New Hampshire, by its Selectmen, Michael Priore, John Reinfuss, and Ralph Southwick, all of Kingston in the County of Rockingham, and State of New Hampshire,

for consideration paid, Grant to Charles H. Haughey and Marguerite E. Haughey, as joint tenants with rights of survivorship, and not as tenants in common, their heirs, successors, and assigns, both of Center Street in the Town of Center Tuftonborough, County of Carroll, and State of New Hampshire, with Quitclaim Covenants,

An easement in, to, upon and over a certain parcel of land, situated Northerly of the New Boston Road, which Road is also known as Rowell Road, and Westerly of that portion of the Pow Wow Pond known as Rowell's Cove and being a portion of the former right-of way of the Boston and Maine Railroad in the Town of Kingston, State of New Hampshire.

---

[5] Maine Real Estate Law, Chapter 6.

The easement is to travel in a generally Northeasterly direction across the land of the grantors from a parcel located Southeasterly of the land of the grantors, said parcel being currently owned by the grantees to the land of the grantees located nunc et futuro on the Easterly side of that portion of Pow Wow Pond known as Rowell's Cove.

Said easement is also given to permit the grantees, their heirs and assigns, to construct, operate and maintain one or more electrical transmissions and distributive lines, including wires, poles, anchors, guys, telephone and telegraph lines and poles and appurtenant equipment in, over, upon and across the subject premises and is also given to permit the grantees, their heirs, and assigns, to construct and maintain a road for the purpose of ingress and egress and it is not to be construed as an easement given to the exclusion of the grantor, its assigns, or to others later granted a similar right."

Easements may be created in probate documents, including wills[6], dowers and partitions, or divisions. This is not nearly as common as it was in the past. In searching records for access to property, especially tracts which appear to be landlocked, frequently a right-of-way will be found in a probate record if the particular tract in question originated in a partition of the land in the estate. Many of these have been omitted from subsequent transfers of the property, but still legally exist.

---

[6] An easement may be created by a reservation in a will. Bolomey v. Houchins (Mo. App) 227 SW2d 752.

... And also a privilege of passing and repassing at the front door, & up and down the chamber and cellar .... with the privilege of passing from the house to the road. Also and one third part of the well, with liberty to pass and repass in some convenient place to and from the same. And also a privilege to pass and repass from the house to the barn, and one third part of the cow yard. Also a privilege to pass and repass from the said yard to her pasture.

Copy from a 1786 widow's allowance, or dower, giving
easements in certain parts of the estate.

Third — I give, bequeath and devise to my son William C. Noyes the one undivided half part of my home farm in said Atkinson and the one undivided half part of my pasture in Haverhill Mass. which I now own in common with him, also Fifty acres of my Great Woods so called, to be set off on the westerly side of said wood lot by a line parallel to the line dividing said lot from the lot he bought of Ground(?) of Clark Esq. reserving to my said wife the use improvement and income with the right to take off wood & timber as herein before stated he the said William C. Noyes paying all taxes which may be assessed on the same, and making all necessary repairs on the buildings and fences on said estate after my decease so long as my wife may live, and reserving a right of way by my buildings where I now live to the other part of my Great Woods so called through all the paths opened to the same, for the purpose of carrying off whatever it may be necessary to remove from said wood lot —

... and reserving a right of way by my buildings where I now live to the other part of my " Great Woods " so called through all the paths opened to the same, for the purpose of carrying off whatever it may be necessary to remove from said wood lot.

Copy from a 1784 partition of land in an estate. A right-of-way is appurtenant to the parcel set off.

In an article entitled *Easement Draftsmanship and Conveyancing*,[7] Robert Kratovil identified:

"the modes of creating private easements, other than by implication or prescription:

1. Formal grant

2. Reservation or exception in a conveyance of land

3. Covenant

4. Unsealed agreement based on valuable consideration

5. Conveyance by reference to a plat which depicts easements

6. Conveyance referring to a recorded declaration of easements

7. Deed of conveyance otherwise sufficient to convey fee title but which includes language construed to reduce the estate granted to a mere easement

8. Mortgage containing grant or reservation of easement, where such mortgage is subsequently foreclosed.

9. Informal documents of various kinds bearing little resemblance to formal easement grants, but which are construed as easement grants in the interest of justice, usually to prevent revocation by the grantor."[8]

---

[7] 38 Cal L. Rev. 426, 437-8 (1950).

[8] A Practical Guide to Disputes Between Adjoining Landowners - Easements, § 1.02(1).

RESERVATION OR EXCEPTION. Also very common are easements created by *reservation* or *exception.* [9]

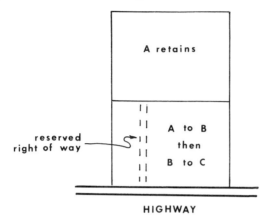

HIGHWAY

*Figure 3.1 A sells to B reserving a right of way to himself over it.
B later sells to C excepting a right of way over it to
landownedby A, or A's successors.*

EXAMPLE:

"The premises are conveyed subject to the perpetual right and easement hereby reserved in the grantor, for the benefit of all remaining land of the grantor, to pass and repass at all times over the granted premises by foot and by vehicle between said remaining land of the grantor and Exeter Road; the location of said right and easement may be made by the grantee, provided, however, that it shall be over a strip of land not less than ten (10) feet in width and shall be so located as to provide convenient access to and from said remaining land of the grantor and Exeter Road."

---

[9] There is a technical distinction between and *exception* and a *reservation*, although the two terms are often used indiscriminately. An exception is the process by which a grantor withdraws from the conveyance land which would otherwise have been included; the grantor merely retains or keeps the part excepted. However, a *reservation* vests in the grantor a *new* right or interest that did not exist in him before; it operates by way of an implied grant. Maine Real Estate Law, Chapter 6.

Mass. 1906. A right of way cannot be excepted from the operation of a deed unless either the right of way or the way itself is in existence when the deed is made. Bailey v. Agawam Nat. Bank, 76 NE 449, 190 Mass. 20, 3 LRA, NS 98, 112 Am. St. Rep. 296.

Reservation of a right-of-way over a deeded parcel.

> "Said premises are conveyed subject to such rights as may be retained by Rockingham County Light and Power Company or its successors in interest to a presently abandoned power line running through the parcel first above described.
>
> Said premises are further conveyed subject to any rights of way which may continue over the abandoned woods road mentioned in the description of said first parcel .
>
> Said premises are conveyed subject to any other rights of way of record."

Example of rights-of-way being excepted from previously described tracts of land in a deed.

AGREEMENT OR COVENANT. An easement may be created by agreement or covenant.[10] Such an agreement or covenant operates as a grant and is construed the same as an express grant. Whether an agreement or covenant runs with the land depends on whether the act which it embraces concerns or relates to the land.[11]

IMPLICATION. The general rule of law is that when an owner of a tract of land conveys part of it to another, he is said to grant with it, by *implication,* all easements which are apparent and obvious, and which are resonably necessary for the fair enjoyment of the land granted.[12]

---

[10] An easement may be created by agreement or covenant as well as by grant. Town of Paden City v. Felton, 66 S.E.2d 280, 136 W.Va. 127.

[11]   If a covenant benefits the land to which it relates and enhances its value, the easement created by it becomes appurtenant to the land and passes with it. Hennen v. Deveny, 71 W. Va. 629, 77 SE 142.

25 Am Jur. 2d § 22.

[12] Maine Real Estate Law, Chapter 6.

Mass. 1948. Implied easements, whether by grant or by reservation, do not arise out of necessity alone, and their origin must be found in presumed intention of parties to be gathered from language of instruments when read in the light of circumstances attending their execution, physical condition of premises, and knowledge which parties had or with which they are chargeable. Joyce v. Devaney, 78 NE2d 641, 322 Mass. 544.

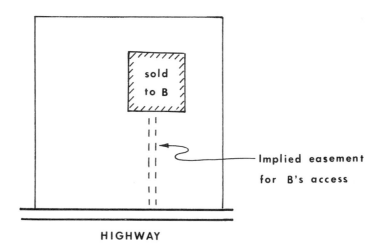

*Figure 3.2   A sells to B without granting an easement for access.
B has an implied right of way across the remaining land of A.*

There are three types of implied easements, according to the three patterns in which they arise:[13]

1.   Easements implied from prior use
2.   Easements implied by necessity
3.   Easements implied from a subdivision plat.

The first category is the implied easement based on prior use of the property:

---

[13] A Practical Guide to Disputes Between Adjoining Landowners - Easements, §
2.02(3).

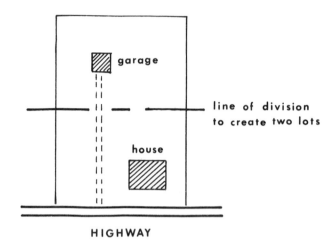

*Figure 3.3 Example of an implied easement based on
prior use of a driveway to a garage*

In Figure 3.3, a parcel of land has a garage at the further end with a driveway leading to it. The parcel is divided into two tracts with the back portion being sold and no mention made of the driveway, or any right of way to the garage. The driveway is implied in the conveyance and may be inferred by the purchaser.

Generally, the following requirements are necessary to justify an easement of this type[14] .

First, the property must initially be owned as a single parcel prior to its division into a dominant and a servient portion. This element of unity of title is also a requirement for an easement by necessity.

Second, during the time that the unity of title exists, the sole owner must use part of the parcel in a manner beneficial to the other portion of the property. Courts often refer to this use prior to division into two or more parcels as a pre-existing quasi-easement.

Third, for the conveyance to give rise to the implied easement

---

[14] A Practical Guide to Disputes Between Adjoining Landowners - Easements, § 2.02(3a).

the existing use must be apparent so that an inspection of the property would result in notice of the use. The use does not have to be visible, however, as courts have concluded that underground sewers, pipes and drains are apparent so long as the plumbing fixtures are readily apparent.

Fourth, the original owner must convey a portion of the property to another person, either retaining the remainder himself or conveying it to a third party.

Fifth, the easement across the burdened portion must be reasonably necessary for the use of the benefited, dominant parcel to justify the conclusion that the parties had the implicit but unexpressed intent to create an easement. Generally a use is considered reasonably necessary if it contributes reasonably to the convenient use of the benefited property. If necessity is the only factor, the courts will generally require a higher degree of necessity, often stated as strict or absolute necessity.

Other factors may affect the court's determination whether an easement based on prior use should be implied. For example, a stricter measurement of proof is generally necessary when the easement is in favor of the grantor rather than the grantee. This is because of the rule of construing a deed against a grantor, and in favor of a grantee.[15]

Implied easements, being unexpressed, are not easements of record. Therefore, in searching records, one should be on guard against this possibility. Assembling surveys and assessors' maps to get an idea of the source of various titles may be of assistance in recognizing possible implied easements.

The second category is an easement by necessity. The crucial factor in this type is that the claimed easement is necessary to the use of the proper-

---

[15] Mass. 1926. Use of particular way by grantor before conveyance and by grantee thereafter may operate an assignment or designation of way by necessity. Davis v. Sikes, 151 NE 291, 254 Mass 540.

ty owned by the person claiming the easement.[16]   The basis of the concept is the promotion of usability of the land. If a parcel were actually land-locked it would lose its usefulness.[17]

Usually a right of way comes to mind whenever an easement by neces-sity is mentioned. However, another example is where minerals are in-volved and they cannot be reached without an easement over (under or through) the surface owner's land.[18]

As with an implied easement based on prior use, it is necessary to es-tablish unity of title. Courts have been willing to recognize a unity of title from the distant past even though the necessity did not exist at the time, and even though the easement has never been used.[19]

No easement of necessity can be claimed when conditions causing a parcel to be landlocked are caused by the claimant. For example, an owner with access to a public highway who blocks that way by construct-ing a building across it, is not entitled to an easement by necessity across neighboring property, even if owned by his grantor. Likewise, an owner who creates his own landlocked parcel through subdivision cannot make a claim of easement by necessity based on the previously nonexistent neces-sity to cross land of another.[20]

An easement by necessity will terminate when the necessity ceases.[21]

---

[16] Presence of a second or alternate way onto property is not conclusive proof that an implied easement is unnecessary. McGee v. McGee, 233 S.E.2d 675, 32 N.C. App. 726.

[17] A Practical Guide to Disputes Between Adjoining Landowners - Easements, § 2.02(3b).

N.J. Super. AD 1965. Easement of absolute necessity is predicated upon strong pub-lic policy that no land may be made inaccessible and useless. Old Falls, Inc. v. Johnson, 212 A.2d 674, 88 N.J. Super. 441.

[18] A Practical Guide to Disputes Between Adjoining Landowners - Easements, § 2.02(3b).

[19] A Practical Guide to Disputes Between Adjoining Landowners - Easements, § 2.02 (3b,i)

[20] Ibid., § 2.02 (3b, iii).

[21] Ibid., § 2.02 (3b, iv).

Md. 1945. A way of necessity ceases to exist when necessity for it ceases. Condry v. Laurie, 41 A.2d 66, 184 Md. 317.

However, mere nonuse of an easement will not result in termination.[22]

Some jurisdictions require proof of *actual necessity*.[23]   For instance, Maine courts have long held that no right of way by necessity exists across remaining land of the grantor where the land conveyed borders on the ocean, even though access by water may not be as convenient as access by land. The test is *necessity* and not mere convenience.[24]

The third category is an implied easement from a subdivision plat. When an owner of a tract subdivides in accordance to a plat, a purchaser of any lot in the subdivision also acquires an easement over the streets as laid out on the plat.[25]

Even though the existence of an easement is agreed upon, its scope may vary according to different courts. Three theories exist:[26]

1.   The necessary (or narrow) rule, where the extent of the easement is limited to the adjoining street and connecting streets necessary to give access to the public streets.

2.   The beneficial (or intermediate) rule, where an easement is granted in those streets that are reasonably beneficial to the purchaser.

3.   The broad rule where the purchaser acquires an easement over all the platted streets shown on the subdivision plat.[27]

---

[22] 25 Am Jur. 2d § 105.

[23] A "right of way of necessity" does not arise if there be already another mode of access to the land, though less convenient or more expensive to develop. Jennings v. Lineberry, 21 S.E.2d 769, 180 Va. 44.

[24] Maine Real Estate Law, Chapter 6.

Pa. 1930. Right of way by necessity never exists as mere matter of convenience. Stein v. Bell Telephone Co. of Pennsylvania, 151 A.2d 690, 301 Pa. 107.

Me. 1925. Convenience alone cannot give right of way of necessity. Littlefield v. Hubbard, 128 A. 285, 124 Me. 229, 38 A.L.R. 1306.

[25] A Practical Guide to Disputes Between Adjoining Landowners - Easements, § 2.02 (3c).

[26] Ibid.

[27] R.I. 1978. A sale of a platted lot with reference to the plat will, as between the grantor and the grantee, give the latter a right to use all of the streets delineated on the plat, even though the plat is unrecorded. Robidoux v. Pelletier, 391 A.2d 1150.

ESTOPPEL. An easement may be created by *estoppel.*[28]   The word "estop" means to stop, prevent, or prohibit. Legally, an estoppel is a bar raised by the law which precludes a person *because of his conduct,* from asserting rights which he might otherwise have — rights as against another person who in good faith relied upon such conduct and was led thereby to change his position for the worse.[29]

Case #5 is an example of a right of way created by estoppel.

PRESCRIPTION. An easement may be acquired by *prescription,* that is, by long continued use of another's land for purposes in the nature of an easement. Such an easement stands in all respects on the same footing as an easement acquired by grant.[30]

Historically, the doctrine of prescription was based upon the presumption of a lost grant, the idea being since the use had continued for such a long period of time it must have been based on a grant which had become lost or destroyed.[31]

---

[28] Ohio App. 1969. Easement may be created by estoppel. Monroe Bowling Lanes v. Woodsfield Livestock Sales, 244 N.E. 2d 762, 17 Ohio App. 2d 146, 460 O.O.2d 208.

Mass. 1970. Right of way created by estoppel is appurtenant to land conveyed and is not an easement in gross. Uliasz v. Gillette, 256 N.E. 2d 290, 357 Mass. 96.

Mass. 1950. A way of estoppel is not a way of necessity, and the right exists even if there are other ways, either public or private, leading to the land. Casella v. Sneierson, 89 NE2d 8, 325 Mass. 85.

NH 1981. Where property is conveyed in a deed and one or more of the calls is an abuttal on a private way, there is a grant or at least a presumption of a grant of an easement in such way when the way is owned by the grantor; and it is of no consequence that the fee to the roadway of passageway remains in the hands of the original grantor or his assigns, or that the grantor did not intend to grant an easement, or that the easement is not one of necessity, because the grantor, and all claiming under him, are estopped by deed from denying such an easement exists. 700 Lake Avenue Realty Co. v. Dolleman, 121 N.H. 619.

[29] Maine Real Estate Law, Chapter 6.

[30] 25 Am Jur 2d § 39.

An easement in light cannot be acquired by prescription, but only covenant or grant, Mathewson St. M.E. Church v. Shepard, 46 A. 402, 22 R.I. 112.

[31] Maine Real Estate Law, Chapter 6.

Additionally, easements created in other ways may be enlarged by prescription.[32]

In most states, the requirements for establishing an easement by prescription are the same as for acquiring title by adverse possession,[33] including the following:

1. Use must be adverse
2. Open and notorious
3. Continuous
4. Exclusive
5. Under claim of right
6. For the statutory period

The first requirement is that the use of the easement must be *adverse* as distinguished from *permissive*. If the latter were the case, then the easement would be based on some form of agreement, and the user would not gain title.[34] To be adverse, the use need not be hostile in the strict sense.

The adverse use must have been with the owner's knowledge and acquiescence or it must have been so open and notorious that knowledge and acquiescence will be presumed. This requirement is for the protection of the landowner and assures him a reasonable notice of the need to preserve his rights against the adverse user.[35]

To be "open" the use must be made without secrecy or concealment. A concealed use will not suffice unless the owner has actual knowledge of it. To be "notorious" it is not necessary that the use be actually known to the owner; it is only necessary that the use be such that a reasonable inspection of the premises would have disclosed its existence.[36]

---

[32] Mass. 1838. Easements created by reservation or grant may be enlarged by prescription. Atkins v. Bordman, 37 Mass. 291.

[33] N.Y.A.D. 1968. Adverse possession and easement by prescription depend on same elements but differ fundamentally in that one is based on claim of possession and the other claim of use. Rasmussen v. Sgritta, 305 N.Y.S.2d 816, 33 A.D.2d 843.

[34] Use by express or implied permission or license, no matter how long continued, cannot ripen into an easement by prescription. 25 Am Jur 2d § 54.

[35] Maine Real Estate Law, Chapter 6.

[36] Ibid.

For a use to be *continuous*   it is not necessary that it be constant or made every day; it may, depending on the nature of the use, be periodic or occasional. What is essential is that there be no break in the adverse attitude of the user[37]

For a prescriptive right to arise the use must not only be continuous— it must be also be uninterrupted. This means that there must be no break in the use brought about by an act of the owner; if the owner causes a discontinuance of the use, even for a brief period, there is an interruption and the prescriptive period must begin all over again if there is eventually a right to be created by prescription.[38]   In addition, there cannot be a voluntary abandonment by the party claiming the easement.[39]

Some states have an *exclusive* requirement. This means that no one else can share the use or substitute their use for the adverse user's. Use which is not exclusive but in participation with the true owner, or others, is not sufficient. However, the requirement as applied to an easement is not as strict as for adverse possession of land. It does not mean that all others be excluded from the property; it simply means that other uses cannot exclude or interfere with the easement rights. It also means that the claim cannot be shared by the public generally. If it is, the use may ripen into a public easement rather than a private one.[40] This does not mean, however, that all public easements are highways.

Strictly speaking, however, courts do not recognize a prescriptive easement in favor of the public because there is no identifiable party for the burdened property owner to challenge. Usually if an owner has knowingly permitted the public at large to use the property in an adverse and continuous manner, courts find an implied offer on the part of the owner to dedicate the property for public use. Custom is an alternative doctrine used in some states to achieve a similar result.[41]

---

[37] Ibid.

[38] Ibid.

[39] 25 Am Jur 2d § 56

[40] A Practical Guide to Disputes Between Adjoining Landowners - Easements, § 2.03 (3b).

[41] Ibid., § 2.03 (4b).

The public as well as an individual, may however, acquire an easement by prescription.[42] In fact, many of the very old highways were established in this manner.

As with adverse possession, the prescriptive easement doctrine does not apply against the sovereign as the servient property owner.[43] However, in many instances, the opposite may be possible.

In some jurisdictions it is essential that the adverse use be under a *claim of right.* [44] It is not necessary, in order to establish a claim of right, however, that an actual claim be made; an intent to claim adversely may be inferred from the acts and conduct of the dominant users.[45]

Claim of right is not to be confused with, or equated with, *color of title.*[46] In most states, statutes of limitation requiring color of title in order to obtain title by adverse possession, have been held not to apply to the acquisition of easements by prescription.[47]

Finally, the use must comply with the foregoing requirements *for the period required by statute.* The time requirement varies considerably depending on the state, and may be extended in cases of disability, such as when the owner is a minor, is mentally incompetent, is out of the country, in prison, or is a reversioner.[48]

DEDICATION. Easements are often created by dedication, as in the case of streets in a subdivision. Dedication may be broadly defined as "the devotion of land to a public use by an unequivocal act of the owner of the fee manifesting an intention that it shall be accepted and used presently or in

---

[42] Piper v. Voorhees, 155 A 556; 130 Me. 305 (1931).

[43] Unless allowed by statute an easement, ordinarily, cannot be acquired by prescription against the government, federal or state, or a subdivision thereof. 28 C.J.S., § 9.

[44] The term "claim of right" means no more than a user "as of right," that is, without recognition of the rights of the owner of the servient estate. Andrezejczyk v. Advo System, Inc., 146 Conn. 428, 151 A.2d 881.

[45] 25 Am Jur 2d § 52.

[46] Color of title is a paper writing which purports to convey land but fails to do so. Carrow v. Davis, 248 NC 740, 105 SE2d 60.

[47] 25 Am Jur 2d § 53.

[48] 25 Am Jur 2d § 40.
Pentland v. Keep, 41 Wis. 490

the future for such public use." While dedication gives the public the right of passage, it does not burden the municipality with the duty of maintenance unless the municipality accepts the dedication. Acceptance is a separate event.

Unlike a conveyance in fee, the owner of dedicated property retains ownership of the fee under the dedicated land. However, an offer of dedication is not inconsistent with an intent to convey a fee out to the center line of the road. In other words, a property owner may dedicate a portion of his land for use by the travelling public and, by conveying lots abutting the dedicated road, convey the fee underneath the road.[49]

EMINENT DOMAIN. Eminent Domain is generally defined as the power of the nation or a sovereign state to take, or to authorize the taking of, private property for a public use without the owner's consent, conditioned upon the payment of just compensation.[50]   It is accomplished through the process of condemnation. A well-settled rule is that where land is taken for a public use, unless the fee is necessary for the purposes for which it is taken, the condemnor acquires only an easement in the absence of a statutory provision to the contrary.[51]
In the absence of a statute expressly providing for the acquisition of the fee, or a deed from the owner expressly conveying the fee, when a highway is established by the direct action of the public authorities, the public acquires merely an easement of passage, the fee title remaining in the landowner.[52]

When a railroad company takes by eminent domain a strip of private land upon which to lay its tracks and operate its cars, it acquires ordinarily only an easement in the land so taken. The rule applies to a right of way for main tracks and for necessary sidetracks, chutes, yards, storage places, and the like. Thus, when a railroad corporation acquires land under a general authority to enter and take possession of it, or to appropriate it, or otherwise simply to take it for its own purposes, whether upon payment of compensation, it acquires only an easement in the land, to use for railroad

---

[49] Creation And Termination Of Highways in New Hampshire
[50] 26Am Jur 2d, § 1
[51] 26Am Jur 2d, § 133
[52] 26 Am Jur 2d, § 136

purposes. Sometimes railroads are authorized to acquire the fee in land taken for their tracks, and such statutes have been given effect by a majority of the courts. However, where the statute contains some express provision which is inconsistent with the fee being taken, the court may construe it as granting only an easement although it expressly uses the term "fee simple."[53]

Under the prevailing rule, a condemnation decree granting a right of way for the purpose of constructing, maintaining, and operating an electric current and power, telephone, or telegraph transmission line creates only an easement in the land and grants the exclusive possession of the property only to the extent that such possession is necessary for the erection, operation, and maintenance of the line, including right of access.[54]

As a general rule, in the absence of a statute to the contrary, land taken for school purposes does not vest the fee in the school authorities or district, but only the right to the use and occupation of the land for school purposes.[55]

The uses for which a public park is acquired are continuous and peculiarly exclusive, and it is generally held that either the fee is taken or an exclusive easement which is the equivalent of the fee, except that it leaves in the owner a possibility of reverter in case the land ceases to be used for a park. But it has been held that the title acquired by condemnation for the purposes of driveways in a park is not a fee but an easement.[56]

Generally, in the case of land condemned for canals, ditches, sewers, pipelines, reservoirs, etc., unless the statute otherwise expressly provides, it has been held that the fee remains in the landowner, the condemnor acquiring an easement only.[57]

EXTENT AND SCOPE OF EASEMENTS. Some easements are defined as to location and width in the document in which they were created. For others, it depends upon the manner in which they were created, or even by the intended use of the easement. For example, a prescriptive easement is defined by the use being made while an implied easement may be defined

[53] 26 Am Jur 2d, § 137
[54] 26 Am Jur 2d, § 138.
[55] 26 Am Jur 2d, § 139.
[56] 26 Am Jur 2d, § 140.
[57] 26 Am Jur 2d, § 141.

by the use contemplated by the parties. The location of an easement by necessity may be governed by the use made of the servient tenement, while its width may be governed by its intended use.

A way, if not located, must be reasonable and convenient for all parties, in view of the surrounding circumstances. It must have a particular definite line; the grantee does not have the right to go at random over any and all parts of the servient estate. Additionally, a party having a way by necessity is entitled to only one route and it must be the shortest, most direct passage to the nearest public way so long as the party has a right to a convenient way and has reasonable access to his property.[58]

If a location is not fixed the owner of the servient estate has the right to designate its location, but if he does not do so, the person entitled to the easement may make his own selection of a location.[59]   In either case, the location is determined by the reasonable convenience of both parties, under the circumstances.[60]

If an easement needs to be relocated, the consent of both parties is-needed.[61]

---

[58] 25 Am Jur 2d, § 64.

[59] Mass. 1824. The right of locating a way by necessity belongs to the owner of the land, but it must be a convenient way. Russell v. Jackson, 19 Mass. 574.

N.J. Cir. Ct. 1886. The right of locating a way of necessity is in the owner of the land over which it is to pass. Heiser v. Martin, 9 N.J.L.J. 277.

[60] 25 Am Jur 2d, § 66.

Pa. 1948. Where a right of way is expressly granted and its precise location and limits are not fixed or defined by deed, parties may define location and determine limits of right of way by subsequent agreement, use and acquiescence. Taylor v. Heffner, 58 A.2d 450, 359 Pa. 155.

[61] Del. Ch. 1979. Holder of servient estate cannot have easements relocated, over objection of dominant estate, simply because location and use had become inconvenient to use and enjoyment of sevient estate. Edgell v. Divver, 402 A.2d 395.

An easement may not be relocated without consent of owners of both dominant and servient estates. Ibid.

Pa. 1947. Generally, owner of easement may make changes, not affecting character of servient estate, in manner of using easement, so long as use thereof is confined strictly to purposes for which it was created. Garan v. Bender, 55 A.2d 353, 357 Pa. 487.

Md. 1963. No alteration can be made to increase easement restriction except by mutual consent of easement owner and owner of servient estate. Reid v. Washington Gas Light Co., 194 A.2d, 636, 232 Md. 545.

4. TERMINATION OF EASEMENTS

An easement is not terminated by mere non-use.[1]   However, as there are several ways by which an easement may be created, there are also several ways an easement may be terminated:

1. Expiration
2. Release
3. Merger
4. Abandonment
5. Estoppel
6. Prescription
7. Destruction of the servient estate
8. Cessation of Necessity
9. Eminent Domain

EXPIRATION. Like any other interest in land, an easement may be potentially unlimited in duration or it may be created to last for a limited period

---

[1] Md. 1972. Nonuser is insufficient to establish abandonment of an easement unless an intention to abandon can be shown. D.C. Transit System, Inc. v. State Roads Commission of Md., 290 A.2d. 807, 265 Md. 622.

of time, in which case the easement will expire according to its own terms.[2] Such a defined period of time could be a term of years, or months, or for the life of either the servient of dominant tenement. Where an easement is created for some specified purpose, it expires when the purpose is accomplished. This could be in the form of the happening of a particular event or contingency, or the occurrence, breach, or nonperformance of a condition.[3] An easement by necessity terminates when the necessity for it ceases. However, most easements have a potentially unlimited duration requiring some special act to terminate them.[4]

> "The above described premises shall be subject to a conservation easement to be granted to the Hampton Conservation Commission, which easement shall continue for a period of fifty (50) years from the date of this deed and such easement shall be for the purpose of preserving the above described parcel in its present state and condition, it being understood and agreed, however, that the grantee, its successors and assigns shall have a right to construct and maintain a road upon and across the premises."

Example of a right of way which will expire at the end of a specified period of time.

> "There is reserved to Emedia Beaulieu and Blanche Gauthier individually and not to their respective heirs and assigns, a right of way over the granted premises to and from other land now or formerly of said Beaulieu in the rear of the granted premises, said right of way being 20 feet in width throughout its entire

---

[2] Ala. 1972. Easement granted for a particular purpose terminates as soon as such purpose ceases to exist, is abandoned or is rendered impossible of accomplishment. Trustees of Howard College v. McNabb, 263 So.2d 664, 288 Ala. 564.

[3] Fla. Ap. 1980. An easement does not have to be permanent, but rather an easement may be created which ends upon happening of a condition. Dotson v. Wolfe, 391 So.2d 757.

[4] Maine Real Estate Law, Chapter 6.

25 Am Jur 2d, § 99.

Mass. 1950. An easement may be granted which will terminate on the happening of some particular act on the non-performance of a condition subsequent. Akasu v. Power., 91 NE2d 224, 325 Mass. 497.

length, the Westerly line of said right of way being the Westerly
boundary of the granted premises, and this right of way shall terminate on the death of the two said parties and this right of way
is to be used for a common right of way."

Example of a right of way which will expire upon the death of the parties.

RELEASE. An easement may be extinguished by a *release* given by its
owner to the owner of the servient land; but only if both parties concur.[5]
The easement may be purchased by the servient owner so long as the dominant owner is willing to sell, if it would enhance the value of the servient estate.[6]

MERGER. Since one cannot have an easement in one's own land, as by
definition an easement is a right in land of another, termination is automatic
when one entity owns both the dominant and servient estates. This causes
the easement to *merge* into the fee.[7]

Whether this easement revives when the land is again divided, depends
on the conditions and circumstances at the time. Most courts have held that
once the easement has been terminated it must be created anew if it is later
wanted. However, in a few special situations, the courts have allowed the

---

[5] Maine Real Estate Law, Chapter 6.

[6] In order to be effectual in itself, a release must be executed with the same formalities as are generally required in making transfers of interests in land. Dyer v. Sanford, 50
Mass. 395.

[7] Unity of ownership and possession of two adjoining lots extinguishes mutual
rights of way, as well as other subordinate rights and easements. First Nat. Bank v.
Laperle, 117 Vt. 144, 86 A.2d 635, 30 ALR 2d 958.

Mass. 1821. All easements, whether of convenience or necessity, are extinguished
by unity of possession, but upon any subsequent severance easements which, previous to
such unity, were easements of necessity, are granted anew in the same manner as any other
easement which would be held by law to pass as incident to the grant. Grant v. Chase, 17
Mass. 443, 9 Am. Dec. 161.

Mass. 1876. In order that unity of titles in the dominant and servient estates should-
operate to extinguish an easement, the ownership of two estates should be coextensive;
and if a person holds one estate in severalty, and only a fractional part of the other, the
easement is not extinguished. Atlanta Mills v. Mason, 120 Mass. 244.

revival of the easement.[8]

ABANDONMENT. Although it is uncommon, an easement may be terminated by *abandonment*.[9]   Non-use does not constitute abandonment,[10]   so
that the acts claimed to constitute abandonment must be of a character so de-
cisive and conclusive to indicate a *clear intent* to abandon the easement.[11]
A mere declaration of an intention to abandon an easement does not effect
an abandonment,[12] nor does a failure to repair.[13]

 As a general rule, an easement acquired by grant or reservation cannot
be lost by mere nonuser for any length of time, no matter how great. The
nonuser must be accompanied by an express or implied intention to abandon. However, the nonuser itself, if long continued, is some evidence of
intent to abandon. On the other hand, in the case of an easement established
by prescription, it is not necessary to show an intent to abandon in order to
prove loss by disuse, and it has been held that such an easement is lost by

---

[8] 25 Am Jur 2d, § 114.

 Me. 1973. Once extinguished, easement does not again come into existence upon
separation of former servient and dominant estates unless proper new grant or reservation
is made. Fitanides v. Holman, 310 A.2d 65.

 Pa. 1957. Easement may remain unaffected by unity of estates, or revive upon separation, if a valid and legitimate purpose will be subserved thereby. Schwoyer v. Smith,
131 A.2d 385, 388 Pa. 637.

[9] S.C. 1975. Easement may be lost by abandonment. Carolina Land Co., Inc. v.
Bland, 217 S.E.2d 16, 265 S.C.98.

 An easement acquired by user or prescription may be lost by abandonment or nonuser. Westbrook v. Comer, 29 S.E.2d 574, 197 Ga. 433.

[10] 25 Am Jur 2d, § 105.

[11] 25 Am Jur 2d, § 103.

[12] 25 Am Jur 2d, § 104.

[13] Mere neglect of the condition of a way is not enough in addition to nonuser to
show an abandonment. Harrington v. Kessler, 247 Iowa 1106, 77 NW2d 633.

mere nonuser for the same period as way required to establish it.[14]

A right of way, whether acquired by grant or prescription, is not extinguished by the habitual use by its owner of another equally convenient way, unless there is an intentional abandonment of the former way. The use of a substituted way, however, may be evidence of abandonment if necessitate by a denial of the use of, or an obstruction of, the original way.[15]

As with prescription, the burden of proof is on the person making the claim.[16]

RIGHT TO ABANDON LOCATION. Generally, a public service corporation which has been granted the power of eminent domain and has acquired location by the exercise of this power, may, if it sees fit, surrender its franchise and abandon its location.[17]

One of the fundamental principles of eminent domain is the land taken

---

[14] 25 am Jur. 2d, § 105

A temporary suspension of the use of an easement is not alone sufficient to show abandonment. Chitwood v. Whitlow, 313 Ky 182, 230 SW2d 641.

Mere nonuser of an easement for a less time than that required by the statute of limitations to acquire a prescriptive right does not raise a conclusive presumption of its abandonment. Groshean v. Dillmont Realty Co., 92 Mont 227, 12 P2d 273.

To constitute abandonment of a right of way created by express grant there must be, in addition to nonuser, circumstances showing an intention of the dominant owner to abandon use of the easement. Kurz v. Blume, 407 Ill. 383, 95 NE2d 338, 25 ALR2d 1258.

Mass. 1876. A right of way, whether acquired by grant or prescription, is not extinguished by its owner's habitual use of another, equally convenient, instead thereof, unless there is an intentional abandonment of the former. Jamaica Pond Aqueduct Corp. v. Chandler, 121 Mass. 3.

[15] 25 Am Jur. 2d, § 105

A right of way, whether acquired by grant or prescription, is not extinguished by habitual use by its owner of another owner equally convenient, unless there is an intentional abandonment of the particular way. Adams v. Hodgkins, 84 A. 530, 109 Me. 361, 42 LRA(NS) 741.

[16] Vt. 1943. The burden of proving abandonment of easement is on party asserting such abandonment. Nelson v. Bacon, 32 A.2d 140, 113 Vt. 161.

Sabins v. McAllister, 76 A.2d 106, 116 Vt. 302.

[17] 26 Am Jur 2d, § 145

for a public use shall be devoted to that use within a reasonable time, and this condition to the taking will be implied even though the authorizing statute is silent on the subject. It follows that a failure to devote property taken by eminent domain to any public use whatever may amount to an abandonment unless continued for a sufficient length of time to indicate an actual intention to abandon.[18]

The question as to the extent of the interest acquired by condemnation proceedings has an important bearing on the effect of the cessation of the use for which the property was taken. In that event, if an easement only was acquired by the condemnation of land, the right to the possession reverts to the owner of the fee, regardless of whether the taking was by the state or by an individual or a corporation. Thus, when only an easement has been acquired for the public use by condemnation, if the use for which the land was taken is formally discontinued, permanently abandoned in fact, or becomes impossible, or the land is devoted to a different inconsistent use, the easement expires and the owner of the fee holds the land free from encumbrance. In any such event the right to possession does not remain in the condemning party, but reverts to the owner of the fee.[19]

ESTOPPEL. An easement may be extinguished by the *conduct* of the easement holder, even though he had no intention of giving up the easement. To produce an extinguishment in this way, the servient owner must have changed his position in justifiable reliance upon the conduct of the owner of the easement. For instance, the *apparent* abandonment of an easement could result in its extinguishment: if the servient owner interprets mere non-use of the easement as an abandonment, and in reliance thereon makes substantial improvements upon his land, *to the knowledge of the holder of the easement,* the latter may be estopped to assert his rights.[20]

An estoppel resulting in the termination of an easement can occur whenever three prerequisites for establishing estoppel are present. First, the easement owner must represent that the easement was terminated. This oc-

---

[18] 26 Am Jur 2d, § 146

[19] 26 Am Jur 2d, § 147

[20] Maine Real Estate Law, Chapter 6.

curs if the easement owner acts in such a way that a reasonable person in the position of the owner of burdened property would be justified in believing that the easement was no longer desired. Second, the owner of the burdened property must perform some acts in reliance on the representations of the easement owner. Third, the owner of burdened property must show that he would suffer significant injury were the easement found to continue to exist despite the detrimental reliance he had made on the easement owner's representation.[21]

PRESCRIPTION OR ADVERSE POSSESSION. An easement may be extinguished as well as created by prescription. In order for an easement to be extinguished by prescription, there must be a continuous and uninterrupted *interference* with the easement for the same period required by the statute of limitations for adverse possession.

An easement may be lost by possession and use by one other than the easement owner in a manner adverse to the exercise of the easement.[22] The possession and use must be actual, adverse, continuous, visible, notori-

---

[21] A Practical Guide to Disputes Between Adjoining Landowners - Easements, § 1.05(8).

[22] An easement created by express grant cannot be lost by mere nonuser without adverse possession, but the easement may be barred by a complete nonuser for the prescriptive period with possession in another that is inconsistent with or hostile to the right of such easement. Kurz v. Blume, 407 Ill. 383, 95 NE2d 338, 25 ALR2d 1258.

An express reservation of easement may be lost by prescription; if servient owner should by adverse acts lasting through the prescriptive period obstruct the dominant owner's enjoyment, intending to deprive him of the easement, he may by prescription acquire the right to use his own land free of the easement. Russo v. Terek, 508 A.2d 788, 7 Conn. App. 252.

Del. 1982. Adverse possession by owner of servient estate will extinguish ways-of-necessity provided all other elements of adverse possession are established. Pencader Associates, Inc. v. Glasgow Trust, 446 A.2d 1097.

N.H. 1985. Easement acquired by grant may be extinguished through continuous adverse possession for period of 20 years. Titcomb v. Anthony, 492 A.2d 1373, 125 N.H. 434.

N.H. 1981. Implied private easement may be lost by adverse possession. 700 Lake Ave. Realty Co. v. Dolleman, 433 A.2d 1261, 121 N.H. 619.

ous,and hostile for the prescriptive period.[23]   Similarly, nonpermissive erection and maintenance by the servient owner for the statutory period of permanent structures, such as buildings, which obstruct the use of a right of way, will operate to extinguish the easement. If, however, the act of the servient owner in erecting buildings or other structures on a granted, but unused, easement can be said to have been done with the permission of the dominant owner, the easement is not extinguished by adverse possession.[24] Nor is a right of way extinguished by obstructions, such as fences, gates, or bars, which are removable by the easement owner and which do not pre-clude its use as a right of way.[25]

As with adverse possession, the burden of proof is on the party so as-serting, in the case of an easement, the owner of the burdened property.[26]

DESTRUCTION OF THE SERVIENT ESTATE. A *destruction* of the servient estate usually extinguishes the easement. for example, an easement in a structure, such as a party wall,[27] is extinguished if the structure is de-stroyed without the fault of the servient owner.[28] Another example is where a stairway through a building on parcel A provided access to the upper floor

---

[23] To sustain the extinguishment of an easement by adverse possession generally, it must be shown that the owner of the easement knew or should have known that an ad-verse claim was being made. Philadelphia Electric Co. v. Philadelphia, 303 Pa 422, 154 A 492.

[24] The erection of a fence and the planting of trees and shrubbery on a right of way, which effectually barred it, constitutes adverse possession which, when continued for the statutory period, extinguishes the easement. Nauman v. Kopf, 101 Pa Super 262.

An obstruction under circumstances that might be termed "permissive" will not ex-tinguish a right of way. Welsh v. Taylor, 134 NY 450, 31 NE 896

[25] 25 Am Jur 2d, § 110.

[26] The burden of proving extinguishment of easement by open, notorious, hostile and continuous possession of owner of servient tenement for statutory period is on party as-serting such possession. Nelson v. Bacon, 32 A.2d 140, 113 Vt. 161.

[27] A "party wall" is a division between two connecting and mutually supporting structures, usually but not necessarily, standing half on the land of each owner, and main-tained at mutual cost and for the common benefit of both parties. Maine Real Estate Law, Chapter 6.

[28] Maine Real Estate Law, Chapter 6.

of a building on parcel B. The termination of the easement maybe implied if that building collapses or is otherwise destroyed in a natural disaster.[29]

Similarly, a right of way over a riparian parcel terminates if the servient parcel washes or erodes away.

CESSATION OF NECESSITY. As previously stated, a way of necessity ceases when the necessity ceases.[30] However, if created by other methods, it does not cease even though the necessity for it does.[31]

EMINENT DOMAIN. Eminent domain proceedings may terminate an easement. A servient estate may be converted to uses incompatible with its easements. A common situation is where rights-of-way are blocked or rendered unusable because of a change in the use of a servient estate, such as when a new highway is established, cutting across a right-of-way.

Major highways such as those in the Interstate System or other "limited access" highways frequently sever access roads and sometimes render parcels or portions of parcels inaccessible. Usually when this happens it necessitates compensation in the form of payment of damages. Occasionally an alternative access is provided, or created, even to the extreme of constructing a bridge over the, or a tunnel under, the newly created highway, as illustrated on the following page.

---

[29] A Practical Guide to Disputes Between Adjoining Landowners - Easements, § 1.05 (4).

Mass. 1928. Where one having easement in adjoining wall for support of building removed building, easement no longer existed. Ansin v. Taylor, 159 NE 513, 262 Mass. 159.

[30] Mass. 1857. A way of necessity terminates as soon as the owner of the dominant estate can pass without interruption over his own land to a highway. Baker v. Crosby, 75 Mass.

421.Md. 1977. Way of necessity exists only so long as the necessity itself remains. Shpak v. Oletsky, 373 A.2d 1234, 280 Md. 355.

[31] Mass. 1876. If an easement is created by grant, it does not cease, although the necessity for it ceases. Atlanta Mills v. Mason, 120 Mass. 244.

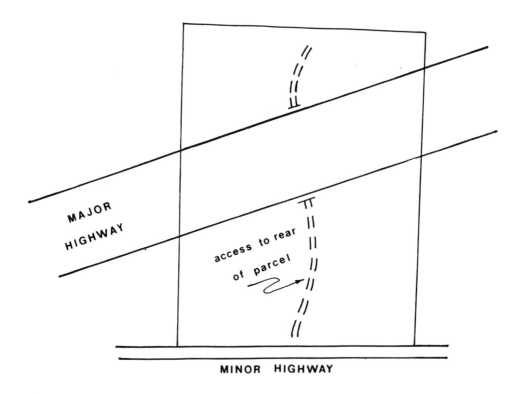

Figure 4.1 Highway cutting across ownership resulting in termination of access to a portion of the property.

5.   REVERSION OF EASEMENTS

When easements are terminated they revert[1] back to the land from which they were taken[2] This is true when an estate less than fee simple absolute terminates, whether it is an easement, a life estate, or some other interest. Occasionally there is a reversionary clause attached to the creation of an easement or other interest, but the usual situation is that reversion is automatic upon termination of the outstanding interest and conditions return to what they were before the creation of the easement, or interest.

EXAMPLE:

"The sole purpose of the granting of this right of way is to insure access by the grantee, her heirs and assigns, to Mohawk Drive in the event of the foreclosure of a certain mortgage recorded in Rockingham County Registry of Deeds in Volume 2069, Page 287. This

---

[1] The returning of an estate to the grantor, or his heirs, after a particular estate is ended. Black's Law Dictionary.

The term "reversion" has two meanings, first as designating the estate left in the grantor during the continuance of a particular estate and also the returning of the land to the grantor or his heirs after the grant is over. 167 S.W. 2d 641, 350 Mo. 639.

[2] Md. 1926. Abandonment of public highway resulted in reversion thereof to owners of soil, free of all public easements. Libertini v. Schroeder, 132 A. 64, 149 Md. 484.

Conn. 1955. Owners of property adjoining highway have right to every use and profit which can be derived from it consistent with easement of public, and soil of highway descends to heirs and passes to grantees as an appurtenant to land adjoining, and whenever highway is discontinued, adjoining proprietors hold land discharged of easement. Antenucci v. Hartford Roman Catholic Diocesan Corp., 114 A.2d 216, 142 Conn. 349.

easement is therefore granted in the condition that the easement, and all rights hereunder, shall terminate and revert to the grantor, its successors or assigns, upon the discharge of said mortgage.

Example of a reversionary clause in a mortgage concerning a right-of-way.

When reversion takes place and boundary lines are involved, one of two sets of conditions arise, Neither of which is simple:

1. Boundaries "go back" to what they were before the creation of the easement. This is not an accurate description of what happens, since the original boundaries never changed: an easement does not serve to change original boundaries of land[3]

This can be a complex situation, since many years may have elapsed since the creation of the easement and conditions may have changed considerably. Also it may be a matter of re-creating property and easement boundaries at the time of creation, which could involve extensive land records research and locating boundaries in existence at the time.

2. Usually boundary lines have changed, or new parcels have been created since the creation of the easement. The chain of events must be determined from the creation of the easement to date, to know what new boundaries have been established

Such a procedure may become quite involved in the case of highway boundaries as will be seen in the examples in the chapters on Highways and Case Studies.

HIGHWAYS. Since highways are a special case, sometimes involving numerous complex issues, they will be treated in a separate chapter. In addition to highways however, any type of easement may be subject to reversion and demand the applications of appropriate rules to define titles and boundaries.

---

[3] Me. 1933. Rights of owner of fee in land on which was located highway were revived after highway way abandoned and land discharged of public easement. Burnham v. Burnham, 167 A. 693, 132 Me. 113.

FLOWAGE. In the case of flowage, frequently there have been camp lot subdivisions created along the shore since the flooding initially took place. These lots now may include some proportionate share of the flooded land which is part of the parent parcel. There have been many cases involving shore boundaries because of this situation, and some states have enacted statutes to solve potential title problems. Basically, however, the usual case is that original titles extended to: 1) the center of a body of water 2) the low-water mark, or 3) high-water mark.

By flowage *easement* abutting parcels were partially or wholly submerged and those which were suitable, subdivided into smaller lots fronting on the new shoreline. If the flowage easement is terminated, and the water returned to its former level, a determination must be made as to the ownership of that land between the original shoreline and the flooded shoreline. Determinations are made based on original titles and ownership, original boundaries, subsequent conveyances and wording in the various deed descriptions. There is never a simple solution, but all ownerships are defined by boundaries in some fashion.(See Figure 5.1)

RAILROADS.[4]   Not infrequently, the parties conveying easement rights to a railroad company will specify what and how reversion is to take place upon termination of the easement. Some railroads did this on a regular basis resulting in reversion taking place in one of three ways, the first two being the most common:

1. Reversion to original grantor or his heirs

2. Reversion to heirs and assigns of original grantor

3. Some formal division to abutting landowners, either to centerline, or some other defined boundary line(s).

---

[4] Pa. 1960. A railroad is a "highway" within rule that a grant of land bounded by or abutting a public highway is presumed to carry the fee to the center line of such highway or easement. Fleck v. Universal-Cyclops Steel Corp., 156 A.2d 832, 397 Pa. 648.

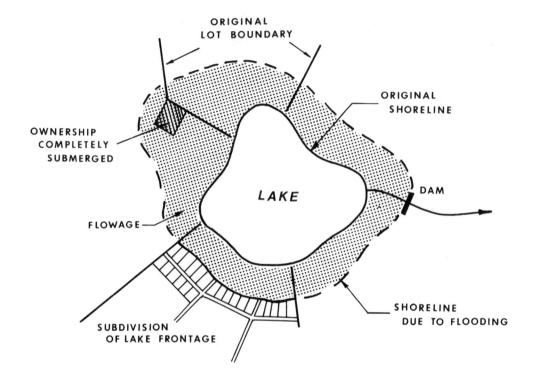

Figure 5.1 Example of flowage easement governing use of upland

A reversion to original grantor or *his heirs* can be a very time-consuming situation in determining if the grantor is still living, and where, or who, his heirs are, or their heirs and so on, and where they reside. Reversion to heirs and assigns of the original grantor demands tracing ownerships forward from the date of the easement to present time in order to identify present successors in title or interest.

Gurdon Wattles, in his renowned book,*Writing Legal Descriptions*, de-scribes an interesting case involving reversion of a railroad right of way.

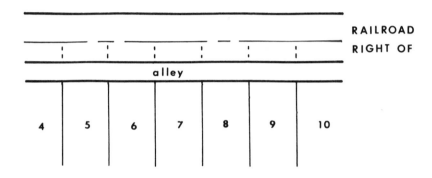

Figure 5.2. Reversion on a railroad

In this case an owner gave a deed to a railroad company for a strip of land across his property and included a reversionary clause in case of non-use for the specified purpose. Subsequently, he sold all the land on one side of the railroad strip to a developer who subdivided it with a marginal alley against the railroad strip. In later years, the railroad gave up its use of the strip but the grantor had to go to court to regain his physical possession of it. In his petition to the court, he claimed his right to the entire width of the strip, but the court decided that in the sale of the adjoining land, the de-veloper (the grantee) acquired the reversionary rights in and to the half of the railroad strip bounding the subdivided land. Because after-aquired title passes to the current owner, this resulted in each lot along the marginal alley acquiring a portion of the "abandoned" right of way opposite the lot.[5]

As previously noted, any easement or interest in land may be subject to reversionary rights. Since easements, according to law, are viewed and treated the same as real property, they should be treated the same as an abutting property owner. There is a status of ownership, and there are boundaries. Both must be determined.

---

[5] Writing Legal Descriptions, Chapter 9.

6. REVERSION AS APPLIED TO HIGHWAYS

Since highway reversions are the most common, most complex and most misunderstood they will be treated as a separate topic. Many of the principles discussed here also apply to other reversions.

Many highways are easements. In fact, highways where the governing body owns the underlying fee are usually rare, and very much the exception than the rule,[1] contrary to common belief. The average landowner believes the municipality, or governing agency, "owns the road," and his ownership stops at some definition of sideline. But discontinue public rights, or have an alteration in road location, and this same landowner wants to know how much of the old road he can claim, or has a right to.

While roads that have the entire public right removed are in the minority, they do exist, and someone owns the fee in what was the underlying bed. More common is an alteration of road location, involving a new taking and layout and a discontinuance or vacation of all or part of the old location. Again, someone owns the underlying fee if the road was constructed on an easement. If the underlying soil was owned by the governing body in fee and it wished to dispose of any portion no longer wanted, it would have to convey it in the same manner as any other parcel of land. Today the conveyance would probably be by deed, whereas in the past there were less formal methods. Additional examples will be found in Chapter 7.

---

[1] R.I. 1948. The public acquires only an easement in a highway, and the fee in the soil remains in the owners of adjoining lands unless the contrary appears. Davis v. Girard, 59 A.2d 366, 74 R.I. 125.

"We the Subscribers Selectmen of Poplin have made a little alteration in turning the highway that leads from Jonathan Beedes to Thomas Cases.............

............by taking out about Seven Rods of land out of the Fellows place now owned by Ezekiel Robinson and for Satisfaction to the Said Robinson we have Given to him the Said Robinson as follows (viz) all the land belonging to the Town in Said highway and range westerly of the following boundaries........."

— April 26, 1806

DISCONTINUANCE OR ABANDONMENT. The term used to denote the termination of the public easement in a road varies depending upon the jurisdiction. The word "abandonment" or "abandoned highway" is frequently used, especially by the public.

"Abandonment" is a poor word to use because legally it has a particular meaning which does not apply to the termination of a public easement.[2] As discussed in Chapter 4, a public easement cannot be terminated by non-use or abandonment,[3] except in special cases, or where the easement was created by prescription.

Discontinuance is a frequently used term, and is defined by statute in many states. Discontinuance denotes formal action by the governing body, changing the status of the public easement, or terminating public rights altogether.

Vacation is another commonly used term which means the same as discontinuance. Both serve to accomplish the same result, that is, terminate public rights in the easement. When this happens reversion takes place automatically and instantaneously.

---

[2] Abandonment is the surrender, relinquishment, disclaimer, or cession of property or of rights. Black's Law Dictionary

[3] Mass. 1942. Intention to abandon is an important factor on the question of abandonment of an easement or other interest in land, and "abandonment" should not be inferred from mere nonuser. Boston Elevated Ry. Co. v. Commonwealth, 39 N.E.2d 87, 310 Mass. 528.

Md. 1972. Nonuser is insufficient to establish abandonment of an easement unless an intention to abandon can be shown. D.C. Transit System, Inc. v. State Roads Commission of Md., 290 A.2d 807, 265 Md. 622.

PROCEDURE. In order to determine how reversion rights apply and to identify the rightful owners and what their lines of separation are it is first necessary to examine the original taking.[4]   This document and its accompanying description should describe the nature of the easement, the width and survey layout (if it was done by survey), and whose land was encumbered, or "taken." This latter information may only appear as a list of damages paid. It may be necessary to review municipal, county or state records to obtain this information. Two typical town highway layouts follow, one based on a survey and one not based on a survey.

> "We therefore lay out the road: Beginning at a stake standing on the town line on land of Lt. John Haley, thence N 23 deg. W 39 rods, thence N 39 W 33 rods, thence North 40 1/2 rods, thence N 6 and 3/4 deg. W 14 rods and 18 links, thence N 17 deg. W 15 rods to land of Joseph S Lawrence Esq., all the above distances through land of said Lt. John Haley, thence N 7 deg. W 51 1/2 rods through land of said Lawrence to the High Road so called near the house of Capt. J.S. Lawrence.
>
> The above described line to be the middle of the highway and the highway to be TWO AND ONE HALF RODS WIDE."
>
> *—June 8, 1830*

> "We the Subscribers Selectmen of the Parish for the year 1773: have laid out a Publick Highway for the good of the Parish aforesaid and adjacent Towns and Parishes: and by a Vote of said Parish: Beginning at the old way by the Corner of the road above Mr. Danle Sanborn's house and then to run up as said way is Trod by Mr. Abner Shepards house to the town line: Said road is two rods wide."
>
> *— March ye 12th 1774*

After the original layout has been identified it is then necessary to determine if any alterations have been made. To do this it may be necessary to search the records forward to date.

---

[4] Me. 1978. A public way can be established by any of three recognized methods: by prescriptive use, by the statutory method of laying out and accepting a way, or by dedication and acceptance. State v. Beck, 389 A.2d 844.

"We have widened and straightened the highway as follows:-

Beginning at the westerly corner of John Wilson, Jr. Blacksmith shop thence running N 85 deg. W 13 rods on Jeremiah Sawyer's land same course on John Watson's 39 rods, thence N 70 deg. W on said Watson's land 10 1/2 rods, thence N 60 deg. W on said Watson's land 15 rods opposite said Watson's Joiners shop.

Said courses to be the north side of said road and the old bounds for the south side of said road."

Example of an alteration of an existing road, February 15, 1834

When all road activity has been accounted for, it is then necessary to search the ownerships under or adjacent to the easement in question. This means the landowners encumbered must be traced forward to determine who the owners presently are. At a minimum, the subject parcel must be searched for the entire period.

Since easements do not cause a change in boundaries, it is necessary to determine boundary location prior to the creation of the easement and then apply the easement on top of the underlying property (ies). Any parcels created after the easement came into being must be treated separately and rules applied depending on the circumstances and the wording of the conveyance(s). Original boundaries remain as they were, new boundaries are created as new parcels are created.

PRESUMPTION OF LAW. The principle recognized almost everywhere, either as a general rule of construction or as a rebuttable presumption, is that if land abutting on a highway (meaning public streets, alleys and roads) is conveyed by a description apt or effective to cover it, and the grantor owns the fee to the center of the highway, the grantee takes title to the center line[5]

---

[5] This means center line of the *easement* and not centerline of the traveled portion, as is sometimes believed.

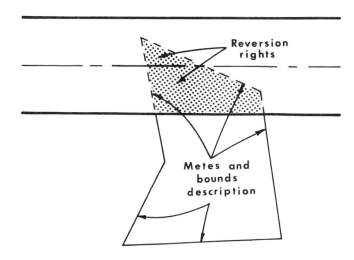

Figure 6.1 Reversion rights are determined by property lines that existed before the creation of the street

of the highway as a part and parcel of the grant, unless an intention to the contrary sufficiently appears.[6] The common belief, because of this rule, is that all lands abutting highways, roads and streets, if they are easements, own to the center line of the easement. Too often the two qualifying statements in the foregoing presumption are overlooked: if "the grantor owns the fee to the center of the highway," and "unless an intention[7] to the contrary sufficiently appears."

---

[6] 12 Am. Jur. 2d, § 38.

The presumption applies to a judgment on condemnation to the same extent as to a deed of conveyance, Challis v. Atchison Union D. & R. Co., 45 Kan. 398, 25 P. 894; Michigan C.R. Co. v. Miller, 172 Mich. 201, 137 NW 555. Annotation: 2 ALR 11, s. 49 ALR 2d 984 et seq., § 2.

[7] 12 Am. Jur. 2d, § 64. The various rules adopted by the court for construing and interpreting conflicts between calls of description all have for their primary purpose the ascertainment of the intention of the parties.

Too often it can be shown that one or the other of these qualifications exist.[8]   Few roads are ever laid out along a boundary line taking one-half the width of the easement from each landowner.

As an example of the first qualification, consider the following layouts:

> "..........then from Sd tree northerly 6 rods and at ye end of 6 rods it is 13 feet wide on James Youngs land and 20 feet wide on the heirs of Jona Smith Decd............"

> "The line above described to be the middle of the highway and the highway to be THREE RODS WIDE except that part bounded on the west by land owned by the heirs of Jeremiah Rowe, which is to be ONE AND ONE HALF RODS WIDE on the easterly side of the above described line."

> "..........Thence 2° W partly on Simon Robies land and on Josiah lanes land 18 rods to a stake............"

> "..........the way is to be 12 feet wide on Sd Mardens land and 21 feet wide on said Greens land."

> "..........Said 2 rods all to be taken out of Sd Martins land and from thence northerly.............. one rod out of Kimballs land and one rod out of Butlers land............."

The main basis of the foregoing principle appears to be the unreasonableness, generally speaking, of the supposition that in conveying land abutting on a highway an owner intends to reserve, or by the use of any

---

[8] Conn. 1824. The presumption that the fee of a highway between two adjoining proprietors is owned by them equally to the center fails, where it appears that one of them originally owned the whole or greater part of the land. Watrous v. Southworth, 5 Conn. 305.

N.H. 1982. There is presumption in New Hampshire that conveyance of land bordered by street conveys title to center of that street, but presumption may be rebutted by showing clear declaration of contrary intent in deed. Davis v. Lemire, 449 A.2d 1228, 122 N.H. 749.

Vt. 1850. The burden of proof to show that parties conveying land bounded on a highway did not intend to convey to the middle of the street is upon the person so contending. Buck v. Squires, 22 Vt. 484.

usual form of conveyance supposes that he is reserving, fee title to any of the highway area, since it is not likely that that area will be of practical importance to him and it is plainly of importance to the grantee.[9] A further ground sometimes assigned for the rule or presumption is found in the recognized principle that when a monument having width is called for as a boundary of premises, the boundary is taken to be the center of the monument. It has also been said that the rule that the abutting owners hold title to the center of a street is founded upon the assumption that the owners have each contributed equally to the street.[10]

This presumption is a rather strong principle of law.[11] Some courts have said that the rule applies even though the highway is not mentioned in the conveyance. The omission from the deed of any direct mention of the highway does not render the rule carrying title to the center of the highway inapplicable if the description is by reference to a map or plat which shows the highway.[12] Some of the later cases hold that a description by metes and

---

[9] The intention of the grantor to withhold his interest in a road to the middle of it, after parting with all his right in the title to the adjoining land, is never to be presumed. Lowe v. Di Filippo, 12 App. Div. 2d 788, 209 NYS2d 652.

[10] 12 Am. Jur. 2d, § 38.

[11] R.I. 1960. Sole abutting owner of land on either side of abandoned highway was presumed to own fee thereto. Nugent v. Vallone, 161 A.2d 802, 91 R.I. 145.

[12] Me. 1968. Ordinarily a sale of lots by reference to a plan conveys rights in streets and ways shown thereon to both grantee and public. Callahan v. Ganneston Park Development Corp., 245 A.2d 274.

N.J. 1950. Deeds sold from maps are construed as passing title to the center of the street, subject to such easement as may have been legitimately obtained. Wolff v. Veterans of Foreign Wars, Post 4715, 74 A.2d 253, 5 N.J. 143.

R.I. 1911. Where lots are sold with reference to a plat showing a street or way intended for the benefit of adjacent lot owners, each owner acquires title in fee, not only in the lot described by his number and as bounded by the way or street, but also in one-half of the width of the way in front of his lot. Faulkner v. Rocket, 80 A. 380, 38 R.I. 152.

R.I. 1867. Where a plat shows the boundary of a certain lot to be a line drawn between the lot and a street, a deed describing the lot by its number of the plat does not convey title to the middle of the street. Tingley v. City of Providence, 8 R.I. 493.

N.H. 1967. Where lots are sold by reference to record plat showing existing or proposed streets which constitute boundaries of lots, a conveyance ordinarily operates to convey to grantee fee simple to land underlying the adjoining streets and rights-of-way to center line, together with easements to use such rights-of-way as well as others which do not bound lot conveyed. Gagnon v. Moreau, 225 A.2d 924, 107 N.H. 507.

bounds which runs along the highway's inner side line operates to exclude the highway area from the conveyance.[13]   The majority, however, hold to the contrary, and it should be noted that among the latter cases are some which take the position that, except where a contrary intention may appear, a conveyance by description calling for a boundary identical with the highway's inner edge carries title to its center line although the instrument makes no mention of a reference to the highway.[14]   Some courts have decided that ownership extends to the centerline of a street even if stakes are placed on the sideline and called for the conveyance.[15]   Courts have also ruled that ownership extends to the centerline even if the recited area of the described parcel includes only that portion of the lot outside of the highway and including no acreage under the highway.[16]

The rule that a conveyance of land abutting upon a highway the fee of which is owned by the abutting landowners is presumed to fix the boundary in the center of the highway is not an absolute rule of law, but rather a principle of interpretation inferred by law, in the absence of any definite expres-

----

[13] 11 C.J.S., § 35. A description by metes and bounds, extending to the line of the street or highway, although without express reference thereto, but referring to a plat showing such street or highway, carries title to the center thereof. Wegge v. Madler, 109 N.W. 223, 129 Wis. 412, 116 Am, S.R. 953.

[14] 12 Am. Jur. 2d, § 39.

[15] Me. 1878. A conveyance of a lot, describing the sides as of the length they are outside the street, passes title to the middle of the street. Oxton v. Groves, 68 Me. 371, 28 Am. Rep. 75.

Me. 1981. A conveyance to or by the sideline of a public street gives rise to the rebuttable presumption that grantor intended to convey title to the center of the street unless a contrary intent is indicated; however, that presumption does not apply when the land is bounded by a private way not dedicated to public use. Franklin Property Trust v. Foresite, Inc., 438 A.2d 218.

A reference to sideline of highway as boundary line is not sufficient to reserve an interest in land under the highway. Grunwaldt v. City of Milwaukee, 151 N.W.2d 24, 35 Wis.2d 530.

[16] 11 C.J.S., § 35. Where a survey gives the dimensions and quantity of the land conveyed exclusive of the public way, it does not operate to destroy the presumption that the fee to the roadbed was conveyed; for the reason that such dimensions and quantity of the usable land is ordinarily deemed by the purchaser of paramount importance in determining its availability for the uses designated by him. Van Winkle v. Van Winkle, 77 N.E. 33, 184 N.Y. 193, 204, affirming 89 N.Y.S. 26, 95 App. Div. 605.

sion of intention, for the purpose of finding the true meaning of the words used.[17] The question of where the boundary is to be fixed in relation to the center of the highway depends on the intention of the grantor, which is to be ascertained from the language used in the conveyance construed in the light of the surrounding circumstances.[18] In the case of ambiguity, the construction must favor the grantee.[19]

Application of the rule of construction which carries title to the center line of the highway, if the grantor owns such, will result in the grantee's taking title to the whole of the abutting highway area if the conveyance is one of parcels lying opposite each other and on both sides of the highway. But even though the grantor owns the land on both sides of the highway, the grantee ordinarily acquires title no farther than to its center line if the premises conveyed lie wholly on one side.[20]

If the highway is established on the margin of a tract of land, and in that location lies entirely on such tract, a grantee of the tract, or part thereof bounded on the highway, takes title to the farther edge of the highway unless an intention to the contrary sufficiently appears.[21]

It is possible to convey a parcel without conveying any of the fee under the highway, however the language in the conveyance must be clear enough to leave no question about the intent. Being bounded by a road or running "along said road," do not exclude the road. "Along the east side of said road," and "side line of said road" may or may not exclude the road, depending on other circumstances and court decisions of the particular state. "Excepting the road" and "excluding the road" would seem to be clear, but

---

[17] 12 Am. Jur. 2d, § 39.

[18] 12 Am. Jur. 2d, § 40.

Where it clearly appears from the whole instrument, in conjunction with surrounding circumstances, that the grantor intends to reserve the fee in the highway or street, such intent will be given effect. Nashville v. Lawrence, 153 Tenn. 606, 284 SW 882, 47 ALR 1266.

[19] 11 C.J.S., § 35.

Matter of Ladue, 23 N.E. 465, 118 N.Y. 215; Van Winkle v. Van Winkle, supra.

Slight evidence of intention to exclude the street would have the effect of doing so. Palmer v. Mann, 201 N.Y.S. 525, 206 App. Div. 484, reversing 198 N.Y.S. 548, 120 Misc. 396, affirmed 143 N.E. 765, 237 N.Y. 616.

[20] 12 Am. Jur. 2d, § 42.

[21] Ibid.

may not necessarily be.[22]

In order to except the underlying fee in a road or street there must be definite statements showing a clear intention to exclude the road.[23]   Unless the deed clearly states that the road is excluded, or clearly indicates so by its language, the conveyance is to the center line of the road, provided the grantor owns the bed, or if not, to whatever extent he does own.

---

[22] A reservation "excepting the roads laid out over the land" does not exclude the bed of the street from the operation of the presumption, as the phrase is construed to be a reservation of the public easement only. Peck v. Smith, 1 Conn. 103.

Me. 1892. Where a farm was divided into two parts by a town road, which ran through it, a deed to the farm "reserving the town road" did not reserve the fee of the road, but only its use. Day v. Philbrook, 26 A. 999, 85 Me. 90.

[23] Nashville v. Lawrence, supra.

7.   RULES FOR LOCATING AND DEFINING REVERSIONS

The ownership lines in a street or highway are determined by the owner-ship lines as they existed before the dedication or creation of the road ease-ment. Brown, Robillard and Wilson states that the problem of apportioning the limits of ownership based on the presumption that fee to the center line of the street is conveyed is sparsely found in the court records.[1]   Within subdivisions, where the limits of private ownership are seldom defined, the problem becomes complex on curved and irregular streets. The following rules, partially based upon the customs of surveyors and a few court cases, represent the accepted practice.

BASIC RULE. The basic rule is that, unless a deed or map indicates other-wise, reversion rights extend from the street termini of the property lines to the center line of the street in a direction that is at right angles to the center line of the street. Direct prolongation of the lot line to the center line of the street is not generally accepted method, although some states adhere to that rule. In Kansas[2] and Oklahoma[3] division is made the same as for accretion to rivers, and is by proportion. Figure 7.2 illustrates the problems which arise when prolonging lot lines.

---

[1] Boundary Control and Legal Principles, 3rd Ed., Chapter 8.

[2] Showalter v. Southern Kansas Ry. Co., 49 Kan. 421, 32 P. 42.

[3] Blackwell, SW Ry. Co. v. Gist, 18 Okla. 516, 90 P. 889.

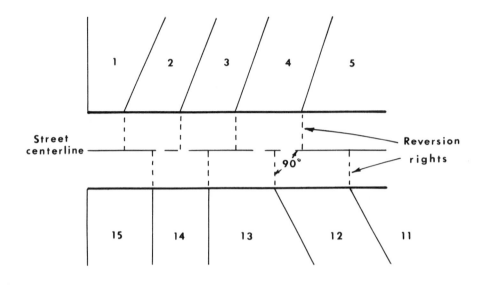

Figure 7.1 Reversion Rights, unless otherwise indicated, are at right angles to the centerline of the street.

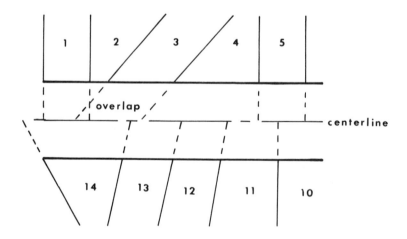

Figure 7.2 The alternative solution, of prolonging property lines to define reversion rights. Problems of overlaps and gaps are likely to occur.

CURVED STREET. Reversion rights on a curve extend radially to the centerline of the street. Radial lines are at right angles to a tangent to a curve. This principle may be considered a special application of the former principle. The example below illustrates the more common application of the principle.

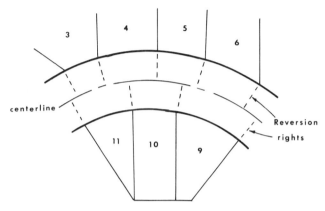

Figure 7.3 Reversion rights on a curved street extend along radial lines to the centerline of the street.

STREET INTERSECTION. Extending lot lines at right angles to the street with ownership to the center of the street results in the following illustration of reversion rights at a street intersection.

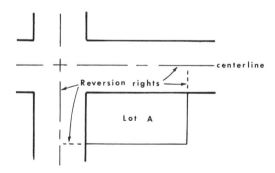

Figure 7.4 Reversion rights at a street intersection.

CURVED STREET INTERSECTION. At a curved street intersection reversion rights also extend to the center line as determined by a curved line. This curve may be simple, compound, reverse or spiral. In any case, ownership extends to the centerline of the street, or highway.

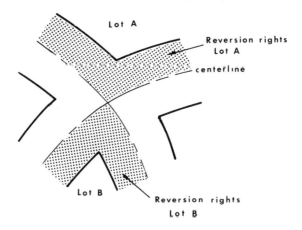

Figure 7.5 Reversion rights at a curved intersection.

LOTS AT AN ANGLE POINT IN ROAD: Reversion rights are defined by the bisecting line in the following example, where there is an angle point in the road. Lot 8 will receive a greater amount of land than Lot 4, even though both lots have equal amounts of road frontage.

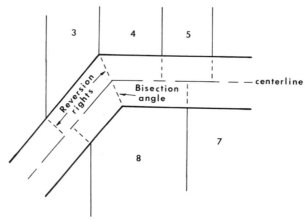

Figure 7.6 Reversion rights at an angle point in a road.

LOTS ADJOINING A SUBDIVISION BOUNDARY. Ownership to the center of the street takes place *when the grantor owned that far*. The following two examples are based on situations where such was *not* the case.

In the first example, Lot 1 in Hemlock Heights and Lot A of Pine Acres are in different subdivisions, the heavy line representing the boundary between the parent parcels. Both parent parcels were created after the road, so therefore ownership of them extends to the centerline.

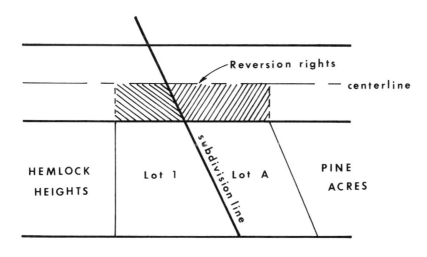

Figure 7.7 Example of reversion rights involving a subdivision boundary.

In the next example, the road cut across the parent parcel and therefore lines of lots created by later subdivision could only extend as far as the grantor's ownership. That ownership did not extend as far as the centerline for some lots, but extended beyond the centerline for others.

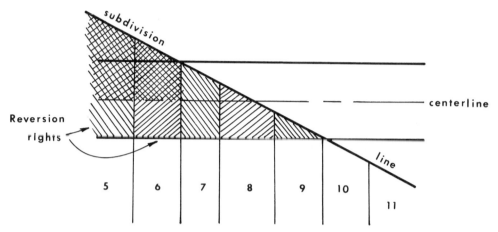

Figure 7.8 Reversion rights of lots along a subdivision boundary which is intersected diagonally by a highway.

MARGINAL ROAD. In the case of a marginal highway, ownership is presumed to extend across the entire highway.[4]

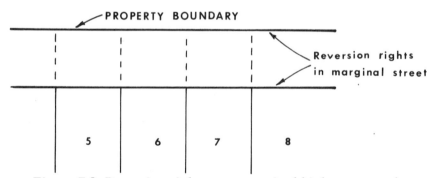

Figure 7.9 Reversion rights on a marginal highway extend across the entire highway.

---

[4] N.J. Super. Ch. 1972. Owner of lot adjacent to marginal highway is presumed take a naked fee to entire bed of the highway. Brighton Const., Inc. v. L & J Enterprises, Inc., 296 A.2d 335, 121 N.J. Super. 152, affirmed 313 A.2d 617, 126 N.J. Super. 186.
    12 Am Jur 2d, § 42.
    Ariz. 1962. Torrey v. Pearce, 373 P. 2d 9, 92.
    Ariz. 12.

SPECIAL CASES. Courts have decided a number of cases dealing with special circumstances and state decisions must be reviewed to determine the courts feeling in these cases. For instance, in New Hampshire, the court decided the following:

> N.H. 1971. Defendants in quiet title action who held deeds to property bounded by the edge of road which ran between property and the ocean, and not by the edge of the ocean, gained title to the land extending to the ocean when town officially discontinued the public road, and master's report concluding that plaintiff, an adjacent landowner who produced recent quitclaim deed containing vague language which might have referred to the property, had no title to any land between the ocean and former boundary of defendants' property was not inconsistent or against the weight of the evidence.-Sheris v. Morton, 276 A.2d 813, 111 N.H. 66, certiorari denied 92 S. Ct. 727, 404 U.S. 1046, 30 L.Ed.2d 735.

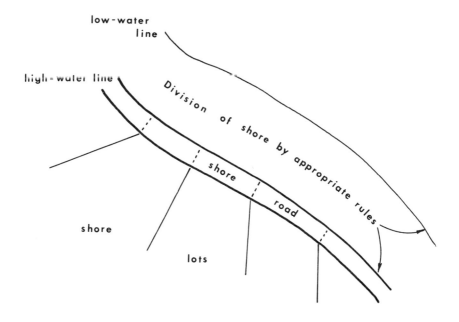

Figure 7.10 Marginal road on a shoreline illustrating division of private ownership.

This case results in two, perhaps three, sets of conditions in the case of reversion. The road itself would need to be divided, either as a whole strip, or one set of rules applied to the near side of the centerline and another to the area on the far side. Then an additional set of rules is needed for the division of the shore since ownership extends to low-water mark.[5]

PROBLEM CASES. There are indeterminate cases if the foregoing rules are strictly adhered to. In the following case a right angle street intersection was altered to form a smooth curve. Additional land was taken from Lot 1 and the public easement vacated for the area no longer needed for street purposes, that is, parts of Lots 2, 3, 4, 5 and adjoining lots (unnumbered). Applying normal rules for the division of the area vacated would result in the boundary lines shown in the following example. Normally, according to the rules, Lot 1 would get area X. In one court case[6] it was held that an area similar to X belonged to the abutting owners who were entitled to road access. Giving the area to Lot 1 does present an access problem for Lots 2, 3 and 4. However, if area X is given to Lots 2, 3, 4 and 5, how should it be divided?

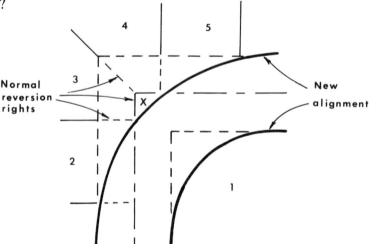

Figure 7.11 Example of foregoing indeterminate case.

---

[5] Nudd v. Hobbs, 17 N.H. 524 (1845).
   Clement v. Burns, 43 N.H. 609 (1862).

[6] 149 Ky. 409.

A single right angle street can also be a problem. The shaded area is best treated with a bisecting line as shown in Figure 7.6.

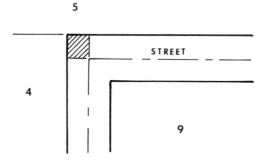

Figure 7.12 Area of reversion on a right angle street.

A dead-end street is a worse situation. Ordinarily, lots 2 and 4 would share the land under the street, each to the centerline. If that were applied here, Lot 3 would not get any part of the street and may have a problem of access.[7]

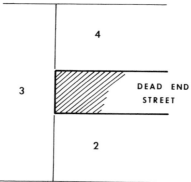

Figure 7.13 Area of reversion on a dead-end street.

---

[7] The Massachusetts courts have addressed this problem. Landowner at the end of a way cannot acquire any fee interest in the way without encroaching on the property rights, if any, of the abutting side owners. Emery v. Crowley, 359 N.E.2d 1256, 371 Mass. 489 (1976).

    Term "abutting," in context of fee ownership of ways after conveyance of property bounded on a way, refers to property with frontage along the length of a way. M.G.L.A. c. 183, §§ 58, 58(a)(i,ii), Emery v. Crowley, Id.

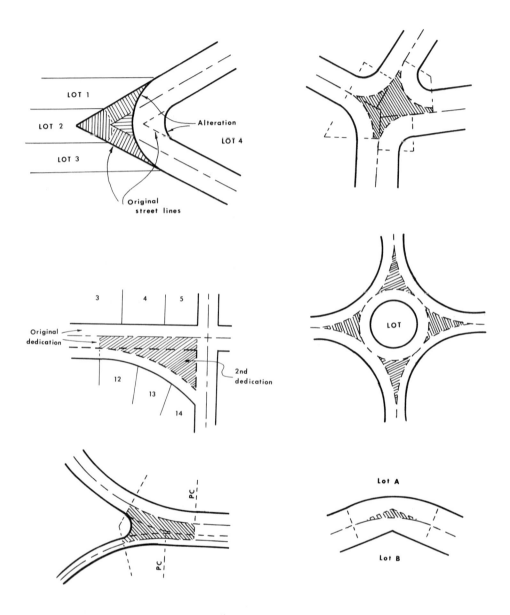

Figure 7.14 Several examples of indeterminate areas of reversion. Title of lots adjoining streets is uncertain as to the shaded areas. (From Wattles, Land Survey Descriptions).

ROAD NOT IN RIGHT OF WAY. Not all that uncommon is the situation where the actual traveled way is found to be either wholly or partially outside of the easement. Some courts have addressed this problem,[8] and it may be necessary to seek court determination in each case.[9]   If sufficient time has passed as required by statute for the creation of a prescriptive easement, then the public may have acquired rights to the traveled portion through use, thereby having title to all of it, the unused portion being part of the easement through the original establishment. In the case where sufficient time has not passed, the public may not have acquired title to the traveled portion, therefore full interest would remain in private parties. If this is the case the governing body would need to be approached about paying damages, a land exchange, or some other means whereby the discrepancy is resolved.

Some courts have stated that it is the road as actually laid out which controls, rather than its record layout.[10]

---

[8] Me. 1898. A deed bounding the land conveyed as on the west line of a highway, where the highway was built four rods outside of the recorded location, conveys land to the limit of the road as laid out and actually used for travel. Brooks v. Morrill, 42 A. 357, 92 Me. 172.

[9] 11 C.J.S., § 36. When a highway or street is referred to in a grant or other conveyance as a boundary, the way as opened and actually used is construed or understood to be the boundary, rather than the way as formerly existing, or as existing of record, or as surveyed for a proposed change , or, in the absence of any evidence to show a different intention, as platted. Johnston v. Palmetto, 77 S.E. 807, 139 Ga. 556; Rosenblath v. Marabella, 3 La.App. 584; Davis v. Monroe, Tex. Civ. App., 289 SW 460; Southern Iron Works v. Central of Georgia R. Co., 31 So. 723, 131 Ala. 649; Winchester v. Payne, 102 P. 531, 10 Cal. App. 501; Hill v. Taylor, 4 N.E.2d 1008.

[10] When a street is referred to in a deed as a boundary, the street as opened and actually used, rather than its record lay-out, is the boundary intended. Falls Village Water Power Co. v. Tibbetts, 31 Conn. 165; Sproul v. Foye, 55 Me.162; Brown v. Heard, 27 A. 182, 85 Me. 294; O'Brien v. King, 7 A. 34, 49 N.J. Law, 79; Aldrich v. Billings, 14 R.I. 233.

Brooks v. Morrill, 42 A. 357, 92 Me. 172. supra.

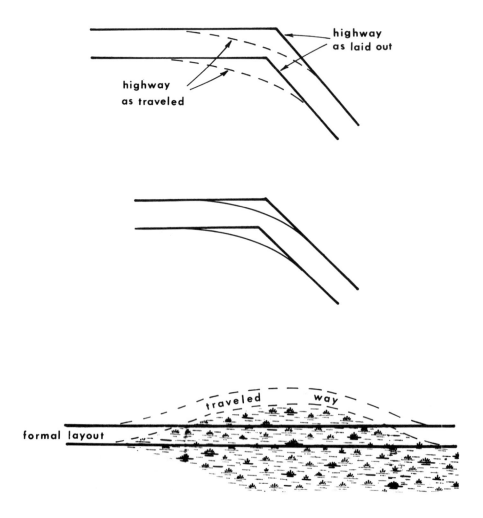

Figure 7.15 Examples of traveled way falling outside of the easement.

DOCUMENTS INDEFINITE OR NOT AVAILABLE. Too many documents are not definite in easement location or in definition. Frequently, roads lack a good description of layout or fail to define the width. This is particularly true of older layouts:

"laid out a highway, beginning at a white oak marked H.I.B., and 4 rods in breadth along by the head of Joseph Bunker his land from thence to the King's thorofair Road. Laid out this 9th of April 1703 by us.
Jno Tuttle, Jere Busnam, James Davis, of the Committee"

"We have this day Laid out a highway on Joseph Halls land, Beginning at Thomas Merrills southwest Corner and so Running Westerly as the fence now Stands as far as Hall's house it contains about twenty square rods of land."

—Dec. 15, 1788."

The State of Maine recognized this problem, and in 1971 enacted the following statute:

§2103.   Lost or unrecorded boundaries.

When a highway survey has not been properly recorded, preserved or the termination and boundaries cannot be ascertained, the board of selectmen or municipal officers of any municipality may use and control for highway purposes 1 1/2 rods on each side of the center of the traveled portion of such way.

It would seem that this is the most logical approach to this type of problem. One cannot do more than act on the best evidence that is available.[11] However, one must be as certain as possible that the best evidence available is at hand. Too often decisions are made prematurely or in haste, as illustrated by Case # 3, in Chapter 8.

---

[11]   N.Y.Ct.Cl. 1963. In absence of evidence to contrary, the earliest known center line of traveled highway is considered center line of highway right-of-way, and when original survey of such road runs single line such line is presumed to be center line of highway. Clark v. State, 246 N.Y.S. 2d 53, 41 Misc.2d 714.

Where the width of a way is not specifically defined in the grant or reservation, the width is such as is reasonably convenient and necessary for the purposes for which the way was created. In such a case, the determination of width becomes basically a matter of the construction of the instrument in the light of the facts and circumstances existing at its date and affecting the property, the intention of the parties being the object of the inquiry. 25 Am Jur 2d, § 78.

SUMMARY OF PROCEDURE FOR DETERMINING REVERSION RIGHTS IN VACATED HIGHWAYS.

1. Procure original documents creating the highway and determine if the layout is easement or fee. These may or may not contain language as to what reversion is to take place in the case of termination of an easement. They should locate the easement and specify its dimensions, at least its width, although sometimes all of this information is lacking. The description should also specify the landowners who were burdened at the time, at least a list of owners to whom damages were paid should be included. The document should also spell out any particular characteristics, such as term or years, restrictions on use, and the like.

2. Determine boundaries and ownerships affected by the layout at the time. Deeds and related title documents must be assembled for this point in time or earlier to know which properties are affected and what their boundaries are.

3. Research records to determine if the layout has been changed. Alteration may come in the form of a re-location of the right-of-way, particularly if obstacles are encountered at the time of actual layout, or in the form of a widening or straightening, or combination thereof.

4. Ownerships must be traced forward to date and related to present ownerships. It is necessary to determine if any parcels have been created by subdivision of original parcels or if there have been any changes in original property lines.

5. Review the discontinuance document(s). There may be special considerations, a partial or temporary discontinuance, or particular wording which would affect the result.

6. Apply the appropriate rules. In the case of problem situations it may be necessary to involve all potentially affected owners, or failing that, petitioning the court for a determination, such as through an action to quiet the title to a particular area of land.

8. CASE STUDIES

The following are examples of some fairly routine problems. Typical of situations encountered with older discontinued highways and elusive or unclear records, they present a challenge to the landowner, title attorney and land surveyor. All of these examples demanded expertise beyond that of the average treatment. Of the five, three were decided by the courts, two of them by the Supreme Court of New Hampshire.

These situations and their analyses demonstrate how important it is to assemble all of the facts before making the appropriate decision. Many problems can be avoided through adequate research of the facts and law important to the case.

CASE # 1:
Who owns the road?

In 1982 a survey was done of parcel B. The surveyor located the remains of an old road between the parcels and, from sideline evidence in the form of ancient fences, determined that the road was two rods in width. In addition, relying on the presumption that abutting owners own to the centerline of an "abandoned" (discontinued) road, he produced a plan depicting the centerline of the road as the boundary between Lots A and B.

A dispute followed and the owner of Lot A blocked off the road, preventing its use by the owners of Lot B. This was critical to Lot B for access to the barn and to back land. Late in 1982 the owner of Lot B brought suit against the owner of Lot A to quiet the title in one-half of the old road. As a result of the research done for court testimony, the following facts were uncovered.

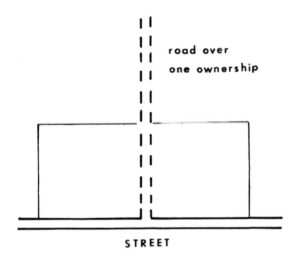

The road in question was laid out in 1742:

"August 13, 1742. a return of an open highway laid out by Selectmen and a committee chosen, beginning at a highway that leads from Salisbury through South Hampton to Kingston near ye Meeting house in said town, beginning first at ye passway 2 rods westerly of Timothy Johnsons line at a stake in said Johnsons line at ye foot of ye hill 2 rods in width westerly across said Timothys land to a stake near the brow of the hill from thence across Thomas Morrills land 2 rods in width & across lands of Joseph Maxfield, John Ordway, Moses Bartlett, Samuel Flanders, Jacob Fowler to back River so called and from Said River on Asa Browns land and land of Abraham Brown to the highway that leads from Salisbury through a part of South Hampton called ye Poock."

The road at the area in question was actually laid out entirely on land of Timothy Johnson.

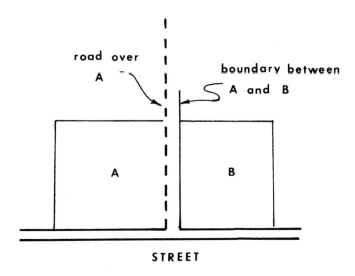

In 1842, the Town voted to close the road.

To understand all the events relating to the road, comprehensive deed research was done on both chains of title. This resulted in the following:

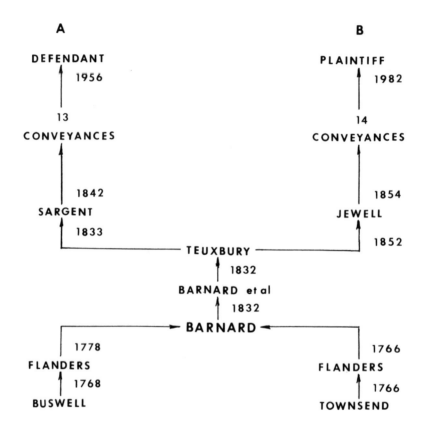

A

DEFENDANT
↑ 1956

13
CONVEYANCES

1842
SARGENT
↑ 1833

B

PLAINTIFF
↑ 1982

14
CONVEYANCES

1854
JEWELL
↑ 1852

————— TEUXBURY —————
↑ 1832
BARNARD et al
↑ 1832
► BARNARD ◄

1778
FLANDERS
↑ 1768
BUSWELL

1766
FLANDERS
↑ 1766
TOWNSEND

A merger of title took place as follows:

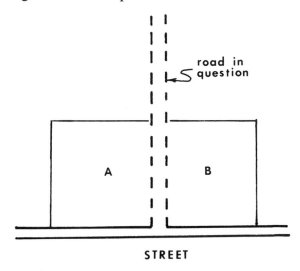

Since parcels A and B are in one ownership, there are no longer two parcels separated by a road, but one parcel with a road across it.

The next important step was to examine the descriptions of the outsales from this one parcel. This took place as follows:

Westerly parcel:

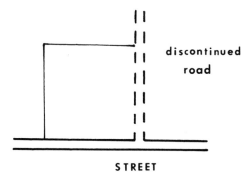

. . ."bounded easterly by the road from the meetinghouse to the peak".

Easterly parcel::

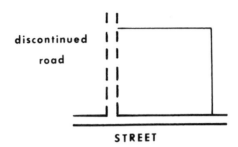

discontinued
road

STREET

... "bounded westerly by the road from the meetinghouse to Kensington".

The road was in existence at the time the above two parcels were created, not being discontinued until some years later, in 1842. Examination of the chains of title did not disclose any alterations in the road; review of town records did not reveal any changes in road status except the 1842 discontinuance.

Since the parcels in question originated from a common source parcel with a road easement over it and used the road as a common boundary between them, it remains to review where the actual boundary lies in relation to that road.

The presumption is that abutting owners take to the centerline of an easement upon discontinuance *as long as the grantor owns that far and unless the contrary appears.* In this case the grantor did own the land and the contrary did not appear. Since there was no language in any of the deeds to limit the boundary to the sideline of the road, or otherwise the center line of the easement should be the boundary between the two parcels.

The case was tried in 1986 and the court found for the plaintiff. It stated that the boundary between the parcels was indeed the centerline of the old road.

This case is somewhat interesting in that knowledge of the entire history of the title is necessary to realize that a merger of title took place when the road was an open, public easement. If that had not been the case, all other facts being the same, the boundary would not have been the centerline, but would have been the easterly sideline, as originally laid out over Johnson's land. The easement would revert and would not alter the boundary. The change in boundaries took place because of a merger of title and the creation to two new parcels.

CASE # 2:
Who owns the land?

In 1971, a major subdivision was done abutting a State highway, which was a primary road in the state. In 1988, a survey was done on Lots 1, 2 and 3, and in doing so it was necessary to determine the ownership of that portion of land between the lots and the highway.

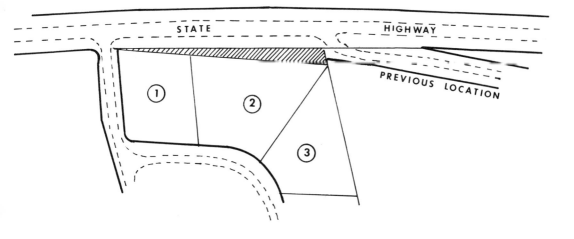

It seemed a simple matter to consult the State Highway Department and inquire about the ownership, or determine who they identified as owners when they changed the location of the road. Before doing that, however, background research was done in order to get an idea of the details of the situation.

1 . Early maps of the town were located in an attempt to determine how long the original road had been in existence. Maps dating back to 1774 showed the road in question.

2 . Highway layouts for the town were researched in the town records and the following was found:

> "Return of the Publick Highway laid out in the year 1792
>
> First beginning at the town line the south side of the river where the way is now open and passable and running in the same path or way as it is now opened and passable to Andrew Folsoms House and then running on the Line between 37 & 42 to the corner tree marked 30 & 37 and then into the Road that is cut and make passable and then by Nathl Ambrose Barn by Peter Warrens House and to Road and to be 3 rods wide."

This layout, while not very definitive, at least gave a width of 3 rods (49.5 ft.).

3 . A copy of the present layout by the State shows the road as being 83 or 100 feet wide, depending on location and its position at the area in question is the result of an alteration. Discussion with the State right-of-way department resulted in there having been an alteration in 1954.

4 . Deed research was done to determine what land was conveyed to the State for highway purposes.

> "Parcel # 1 - All the land belonging to the Grantor that comes within a distance of fifty (50') feet measured Easterly of the center line as shown on a plan on file in the records of the Department of Public Works & Highways; and to be filed in the Registry of Deeds; between land now or formerly of Leslie Moody on the South near Station 57+00, and other land of the Grantor on the North near Station 65+00."

> "Parcel # 2 - All the land belonging to the Grantor that comes within a distance of fifty (50') feet measured Easterly and fifty (50') feet measured Westerly from said center line, between land now or formerly of Earl A. and Lela H. Lawrence on the South near Station

62+50, and land now or formerly of Almond O. Bryant on the North near Station 75+50."

It was determined that the State obtained fee title to a 50-foot strip from Station 57+00 to Station 75+50, along with other land.

5. In discussion with the State right-of-way department, it was found that the State released all their rights to the Town for all interest between Station 65+50 and Station 81+50.

6. Contact with the Town disclosed that they had never discontinued the "old highway," or had given up any of their rights.

The application of the rule of presumption of conveyance to centerline would give the present owners title to the area in question. To be certain, the attorney for the previous grantors (a corporation) was contacted and it was found that (1) the corporation had been dissolved, (2) the officers had intended to convey everything they owned, and (3) they were available and willing to execute a deed to all right, title and interest, if any, in any land that remained. Once that was accomplished, the survey was completed.

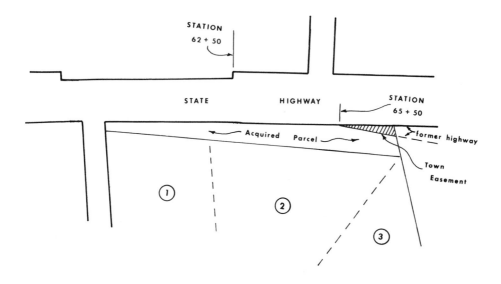

CASE # 3:
How much research is necessary?

In 1980, a subdivision was done of a tract of land which was a remainder parcel due to the alteration of a public highway.

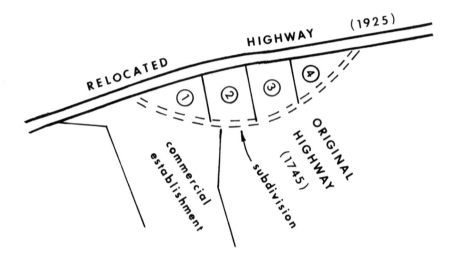

In doing the subdivision, the surveyor obtained a copy of the current highway plans and inquired of the town road agent as to the status of the old highway. He was informed that the road was "abandoned" and as a result, he assumed title to the centerline. Sideline location and width were determined from the existence of the parallel stone fences which were obviously very old and were approximately two rods apart.

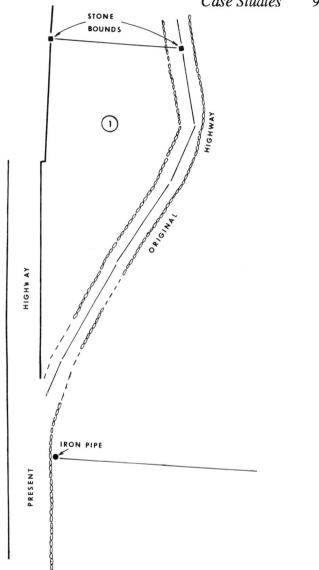

The owner of Lot 1, having been deeded one-half of the old road, decided to exercise his right in preventing any one else from using that portion.
He had no use for it since his access was from the new road. The problem
that arose, however, was that in blocking off part of the old road he inter-

fered with the access to the commercial establishment on the opposite side of the old road. This owner decided to investigate his rights, and instructed his surveyor to "do what was necessary" to determine all the facts available. Research into the problem produced the following:

1.   State highway records indicated that the road was altered in 1925 when the State widened and straightened the route and left a portion of the old road outside of the new right of way. The parcel of land later subdivided was that which was severed from the owner on the westerly side, who still owned land on the westerly side of the new road. Discussion with State officials resulted in the conclusion that the Town was the only entity which had an interest in, or jurisdiction over, the old road.

2 . Town records were examined from 1925 to date to determine if there was any discontinuance or other action on the old road. A discontinuance was found in 1937 for a portion of the old road about one-half mile to the north, but nothing was found relative to the section of road in question.

> "warrant to discontinue the portion of old dirt road now on westerly side of Route # 108 and connected at both ends to Route 108 and lying South of residence of E.G.W. Currier."

> "voted to close the portion of old dirt road now on westerly side of Route No. 108 and connected at both ends to Route 108 and lying south of residence of E.G.W. Currier. March 9, 1937"

3 . Town highway layouts were researched and it was found that the original road was laid out in 1745. To do this, since no one knew how long the road had existed, except that it was "very old," required that the chains of title for both easterly and westerly parcels be traced back for reference to the road and to determine "when the road was *not* there."

The parcels were traced back to 1712 and 1718, respectively.

After the "window of time" was identified, town highway layouts were reviewed for the layout. The point in time was a very important item in this case for two reasons. The town was formerly part of another town until 1738. If the layout occurred prior to that year, it would be found in the parent town's records. Secondly, the road runs through eight towns, and the layout could be found in all or any one of the eight towns, their parent towns, or State or County records, since several towns are involved. As it turned out, the layout in question was found in the present town records in 1745:

> "August the 6th day 1745 then laid out by us the Subscribers Select Men a high way on the South Side of Trickling falls bridge & Running from thence Southerly to a heape of Stones & from thence Southerly to within three rods due west from the west ende of Theophelus griffins house two Rods wide on each side of the Senter of the now troden path and so Running as far as the town Ship Shall Extend & this is the return we make of Sd way Elisha Sweet Elisha winslo John honton   Selectmen"

4 . The deed descriptions presented a new fact that was an important consideration. The source parcels of the two lots in question were conveyed in 1712 and 1718, calling for the front lot lines being "2 rods easterly and westerly of the old path." This explains why the road was laid out in 1745 as 4 rods wide. If the reserved roadway and the "old path" were not made part of the conveyances, then the fee to this 4-rod strip may still rest with the town. If that is true, and the 1745 road was laid out on that strip, then neither lot may be entitled to any part of it by reversion, since the road is not an easement, but a road laid out over a fee strip.

CASE # 4:
When is a road not a road?
Avery v. Rancloes, 459 A.2d 622, 123 N.H. 233.

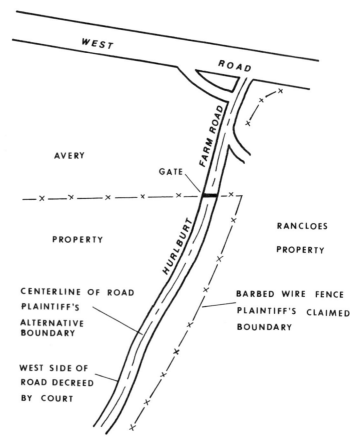

From the judgment:

The plaintiff, Gloria R. Avery, brought a bill in equity to establish her title to certain land in Clarksville. The defendants, Frank Rancloes and his wife, Glenna Rancloes, are the owners of property which is contiguous to the plaintiff's property. The parties' dispute concerns the proper boundary line between their property. The defendants argue that the Trial Court (Dunn, J.) correctly found it to be the westerly side of Hurlburt Farm Road. The plaintiff contends that either the center line of Hurlburt Farm Road or the barbed wire/cedar-post fence on the easterly side of Hurlburt Farm Road is the proper boundary. (See diagram attached to this opinion.) We affirm.

The parties share a common predecessor in title, George W. Anderson, with respect to the land in dispute. On May 15, 1934, Anderson conveyed to Perley Chappel a triangular piece of land described as follows:

"A certain tract or parcel of land situate in the Town of Clarksville, in the County of Coos in the State of New Hampshire, on the southerly side of the highway [West Road] leading from Keazer Corner, so-called in said Clarksville to Beecher Falls Village, bounded and described as follows:
Northerly by the aforesaid highway [West Road]; *Easterly by the highway leading to the Hurlburt Farm*, so-called, and now owned by Perley Chappel; Southerly and Westerly by a stone wall Said tract being triangular in form and containing two (2) acres, more or less ...."
(Emphasis added.)

The following year, this triangular piece of land was conveyed by Perley Chappel to Merle J. Young and Bessie I. Young, the plaintiff's predecessors in title, as part of a larger tract. The physical description of the triangular piece of land included in the larger tract was almost identical to the description in the deed from Anderson to Chappel. Finally, in May 1974, the Youngs conveyed a portion of their land, including the triangular piece originally conveyed by Anderson to Chappel, to the plaintiff. All of these deed in the plaintiff's chain of title were recorded.

The defendants acquired their property, which lies both to the north and the east of the plaintiff's property, directly form George W. Anderson and Annie E. Anderson in July 1958. Their deed is also recorded.

The trial court determined that some time between 1935 and 1958, Anderson and the Youngs probably erected the barbed wire/cedar post fence along the east side of Hurlburt Farm Road. It also determined that the defendants maintained the fence after they acquired their property in 1958. The court found that the fence was built to keep cattle on the property, and was not intended to mark the boundary between the properties. The court also found that Anderson permitted the Youngs to walk their cattle along Hurlburt Farm Road, and also permitted them to install a gate across the road to control cattle and keep trespassers out.

In January 1980, Mrs. Avery, who had purchased her property from the Youngs, closed and locked this gate. She then filed a bill in equity to establish title to the road alleging either that the Youngs' deed to her transferred title to Hurlburt Farm Road, or that she held title to the land by virtue of adverse possession. She claims, in the alternative, that even if she does not have title to the road, that she acquired an easement to use the road because of adverse use.

The trial court rejected these arguments. It held that the boundary of the plaintiff's property was the west side of the road. The court stated that Chappel's deed to the Youngs established the boundary at the west side of the road and that the Youngs had owned no part of the road. Consequently, when the Youngs conveyed the land to the plaintiff, they could convey only what they owned, and thus, the plaintiff's property reached only to the west side of the road. Finally, the court held that the plaintiff failed to prove her claim of adverse possession. The plaintiff appealed.

The plaintiff argues that the court erred in holding that she acquired no part of the road by deed. She claims that, in construing Anderson's deed to Chappel, the court should have applied the general rule that a conveyance of property bounded by a street or highway conveys title to the center of the boundary street unless clearly contrary language appears in the deed. See Duchesnaye v. Silva, 118 N.H. 728, 732, 394 A.2d 59, 61 (1978). We hold that the general rule was inapplicable, and therefore find no error in the trial court's holding.

[1] The rule that a conveyance of property bounded by a street is intended to convey title to the center of the street is based on two presumptions. The first is that the owners of property adjoining the street originally furnished the land for the right of way in equal proportions. The second presumption is that an owner selling land bounded by the highway did not intend to retain the narrow strip of land which constituted the road, and therefore intended to sell to the center line of the street. 6 G. Thompson, Commentaries on the Modern Law of Real Property § 3068, at 669-70 (1962 Replacement).

[2] It is clear that the general rule is inapplicable when we examine the facts of this case. In 1927, Charles Felton, Anderson's predecessor in title, owned the land on both sides of the disputed portion of Hurlburt Farm Road. Until that year, Hurlburt Farm Road was a public road. In that year, the Town of Clarksville voted to discontinue the road. When it did so, full ownership of the road reverted to Felton. See Sheris v. Morton, 111 N.H. 66, 71-72, 276 A.2d 813, 816-17 (1971) cert. denied, 404 U.S. 1046, 92 S.Ct. 727, 30 L.Ed.2d 735 (1972). As the Minnesota Supreme Court stated in describing a similar situation, "[w]hat had been a street would be mere land.... The land which had been a street assumed exactly the same legal status as any other land which had not been impressed with a public easement." White v. Jefferson, 110 Minn. 276, 284, 124 N.W. 373, 375 (1910). See Sanchez v. Grace M.E. Church, 114 Cal. 295, 298-99, 46 P. 2, 3 (1896).

After the Town of Clarksville discontinued the road, Felton had title to the land which had constituted the road and to the land on both sides of it. There was nothing legally to distinguish the land which had constituted the road from the surrounding land. Thus, in 1934, when Felton transferred the entire tract to Anderson, he conveyed one large tract of land which was not encumbered by any highway or easement or a private road.

When Anderson later conveyed part of this large tract to Chappel, the general rule that a conveyance of property bounded by a street conveys to the center line of the street was inapplicable to the conveyance because there was no street or road, legally, and the presumptions supporting the rule were inapplicable.

Nor did the rule apply when Chappel later conveyed the same property to the Youngs, using language virtually identical to that used in Anderson's deed, because Chappel could convey only what they received from Chappel. For these reasons, we hold that the trial court was correct in not applying the rule suggested by the plaintiff.

[3-5] The plaintiff's next claim is that she either holds title to the land west of the fence which runs along the east side of the Hurlburt Farm Road based on adverse possession or that she has an easement to use the road based on adverse use for a period of twenty years. She claims that the barbed wire/cedar post fence was built and maintained by her predecessor, Merle Young, and his son from 1933 to 1974; that the fence was understood by Merle Young and George W. Anderson to be the true boundary between their contiguous land; that a gate on the Hurlburt Farm Road was built and maintained by the Youngs from 1935 to 1974; that the maintenance of the fence was of a character calculated to give notice to Anderson, the Rancloes' predecessor in title, of an adverse claim to the land by Avery's predecessors in title; and finally, that Gloria R. Avery and her predecessors in title, Merle Young and Bessie Young, have claimed all of the land westerly of the barbed wire/cedar post fence, open and notoriously, without interruption for twenty years continuously.

Although the testimony on the claim of adverse use was conflicting, the court found that the fence had probably been built by Anderson and the Youngs together not to mark the boundary between the properties but as a fence to keep cattle in. The trial judge also found that, after 1958, the fence was maintained by the defendants and that the gate was probably built by the Youngs to control cattle and keep trespassers out, with the permission of Anderson. He further found that Anderson and the Youngs were friends and that Anderson allowed the Youngs to walk their cattle along Hurlburt Farm Road, and Anderson also walked his cattle along that road. He held, therefore, that there was nothing adverse or hostile about the Youngs' use of the road or installation of the gate. The Court held that the first time Gloria Avery took action which put the Rancloes on notice of her claim of adverse possession was on January 3, 1980, when she closed and locked the gate.

Both of these claims required the plaintiff to show that the nature of her use, and that of her predecessors, was sufficient to put the owner on notice that an adverse claim was being make to the property. Town of Weare v. Paquette, 121 N.H. 653, 657, 434 A.2d 591, 594 (1981); Ucietowski v. Novak, 102 N.H. 140, 144, 152 A.2d 614, 618 (1959). It is well established that permissive use can never ripen into an adverse claim. Id. at 145, 152 A.2d at 618. Whether a use is adverse or permissive is an issue of fact to be determined by the trial court. Ellison v. Fellows, 121 N.H. 978, 981, 437 A.2d 278, 280 (1981). There was sufficient evidence before the trial court upon which it could reasonably find that the Youngs' use was not adverse, and consequently, we will not overturn its findings. Id., 437 A.2d at 280; see Zivic v. Place, 122 N.H.—, —, 451 A.2d 960, 964 (1982).

Affirmed.

All concurred.

This case demonstrates how important it is to know the history of the road and the relationship between the status of the road and the conveyance of abutting lands. The presumption of ownership of road can only take place if there is a road. In this case, there was no road, legally, when Gloria Avery obtained title, even though there was a physical road. Title cannot go to the center of something which does not exist.[1]

---

[1] Another rule which applies in this situation is that a description is to be interpreted in light of the surrounding circumstances. Part of the surrounding circumstances in this case is the nonexistence of Hurlburt Farm Road as a legal road.

CASE # 5:
Right-of-way by estoppel.
Carmela Casella vs. Robert W. Sneierson & another, 325 Mass. 85.

The plaintiff brings this bill in equity to restrain the defendants from erecting a garage on land over which the plaintiff claims to have a right of way. The evidence is reported and the judge made a report of the material facts found by him.

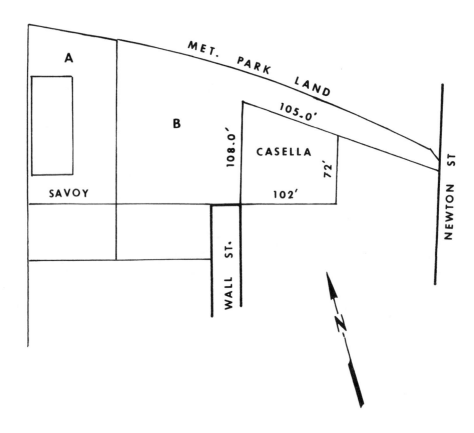

The pertinent facts may be summarized as follows: The plaintiff
is the owner of a lot of land in Waltham on which there is a
dwelling. The defendants own land which adjoins the plaintiff's lot
to the west and to the north and is designated as lot "B" on the plan,
material features of which are shown on page 87, post. The defendants' lot is bounded on the north by a narrow strip of land owned
by the Commonwealth which runs to the Charles River. The southern boundaries of both lots form a continuous line. Wall Street lies
to the south of the lots and adjoins them so that its easterly boundary
if extended coincides with the westerly boundary of the plaintiff's
lot, forming a line perpendicular to the southern boundary of the
lots. Wall street is a private way thirty-three feet wide and is paved
up to the point where it adjoins the land of the plaintiff and the defendants. Beyond the point where the pavement ends "no way had
been laid out, the land being rough and uncultivated and having
thereon grass and stones."

Both parcels of land involved in this litigation were at one time
owned by one Wood. In 1922 what is now the plaintiff's lot was
conveyed to one Durkiwiez by a deed which referred to the property
as "land in Waltham situated on the easterly side of Wall Street, a private way." That part of the description contained in the deed to
Durkiwiez here pertinent reads: "Beginning at the southwesterly
corner of the granted premises at a point in the easterly line of said
Wall Street at land of Hughes; thence running northerly on the easterly line of said Wall Street one hundred eight (108) feet more or less
to a point...." In 1924 Durkiwiez conveyed the premises to the
plaintiff by a deed describing the property in the same words as
those just quoted. In August, 1948, Wood conveyed the land com-
prising lots "A" and "B" on the above mentioned plan[1] to Albany R.
and Joseph G. Savoy, the defendants' predecessors in title. In
October, 1948, the defendants acquired lot B from the Savoys.

In November, 1948, the defendants commenced the erection of a

[1] The plan which bears the date of September 30, 1948, was not in existence when
the conveyances to Durkiwiez and the Savoys were made and was not referred to in
either of the deeds. (This footnote is part of the quoted judgment. It is numbered 1
in the judgement. —*ed*)

garage. The site of the proposed garage is twelve feet from the west line of the plaintiff's lot and fifty feet back from Wall Street. The plaintiff contends that she has a right of way over the strip of property to the west of her land corresponding to a northerly extension of Wall Street and that this way is not only coextensive with her property but extends on northerly down to the river. If only the first part of the plaintiff's contention is correct, then, obviously, the proposed garage would interfere with the plaintiff's right of passage over the way, for it would be located on a continuation of Wall Street at a point opposite the plaintiff's land. The judge concluded that the oral and documentary evidence did not warrant a finding or ruling that any way was created by grant, and that if there was an attempt to create one it was "too indefinite and uncertain to establish any rights thereunder." He found, however, that the plaintiff had a right "both by prescription and by necessity" to pass over land of the defendants along her western boundary from Wall Street to a point opposite the northerly line of her residence. This way, which the judge found to be twenty feet wide and forty feet in length, did not embrace the area where the defendants' garage was to be built. A decree was entered accordingly, from which the plaintiff appealed.

Whether the plaintiff acquired a right of way by grant depends on the effect of the deed from Wood to Durkiwiez, her predecessor in title.[1]   The significant words in that deed are the following: "Beginning at the southwesterly corner of the granted premises at a point in the easterly line of said Wall Street at land of Hughes; thence running northerly on the easterly line of said Wall Street one hundred eight (108) feet more or less to a point: (emphasis supplied). The plaintiff rightly does not contend that she acquired the fee in any part of the way. It is to be noted that the description here does not bound the property "on" or "by" Wall Street. Ordinarily a deed which bounds the premises "on" or " by" a way with no restricting or con-

---

[1] The deed from the Savoys to the defendants contains the recital "subject to a right of way in Wall Street, a private way of record." But his gave no rights to the plaintiff who was a stranger to that deed. Haverhill Savings Bank v. Griffin, 184 Mass. 419, 421. Hodgkins v. Bianchini, 323 Mass. 169, 172.(This footnote is part of the quoted judgment. It is numbered 1 in the judgement. —*ed)*

trolling words conveys title to the middle of the way if the way belongs to the grantor. Gray v. Kelley, 194 Mass. 533, 536-537. Pinkerton v. Randolph, 200 Mass. 24, 26-27. Salem v. Salem Gas Light Co. 241 Mass. 438, 441. Erickson v. Ames, 264 Mass. 436, 442-445. But the rule is otherwise where the deed describes the boundary as being "on" or "by" the side line of a way. Such a description ordinarily indicates that the grantor did not intend to part with title to any portion of the way. Smith v. Slocomb, 9 Gray, 36. Holmes v. Turner's Falls Co. 142 Mass. 590, 592. McKenzie v. Gleason, 184 Mass. 452, 458. Hamlin v. Attorney General, 195 Mass. 309, 312. Wood v. Culhane, 265 Mass. 555, 557. The description in the deed under consideration belongs to this class. Thus Wood's grantee, Durkiwiez, did not acquire a fee to the center of the way and, of course, the plaintiff, whose title stems from Durkiwiez, acquired no better right.

The question remains whether the deed to Durkiwiez, although it conveyed no fee in any part of the way, created an easement of way. The plaintiff invokes the familiar rule that, when a grantor conveys land bounded on a street or way, he and those claiming under him are estopped to deny the existence of such street or way, and the right thus acquired by the grantee (an easement of way) is not only coextensive with the land conveyed, but embraces the entire length of the way, as it is then laid out or clearly indicated and prescribed. Tobey v. Taunton, 119 Mass. 404, 410. Ralph v. Clifford, 224 Mass. 58, 60. Oldfield v. Smith, 304 Mass. 590, 595-596. Frawley v. Forrest, 310 Mass. 446, 451. Daviau v. Betourney, ante, 1, 3.

Although there is some authority to the contrary (see McKenzie v. Gleason, 184 Mass. 452, 458-459; Wood v. Culhane, 265 Mass. 555, 558-559), we think it must be regarded as settled in this Commonwealth that a description which bounds property by the side line of a way is no less effective to give the grantee an easement in the way, under the principle just stated, than a description which bounds the property by or on a way. Gaw v. Hughes, 111 Mass. 296. Cole v. Hadley, 162 Mass. 579. Driscoll v. Smith, 184 Mass. 221. Hill v. Taylor, 296 Mass. 107,116. Thus had Wall Street been in existence along the westerly boundary of the plaintiff's lot at the time of the conveyance to Durkiwiez there could be no doubt, under the decisions just cited, that he and those claiming under him would have acquired an easement of way over it. That Wall Street was not then in existence would not necessarily preclude the creation of such an easement. Lemay v. Furtado, 182 Mass. 280. The estoppel of the grantor to deny the existence of the way "applies as well to a contemplated way if clearly indicated as to an existing street." Ralph v. Clifford, 224 Mass 58, 60. Tufts v. Charlestown, 2 Gray, 271, 273. In the case last cited it was said, "When a grantor conveys land, bounding it on a way or street, he and his heirs are estopped to deny that there is such a street or way. This is not descriptive merely, but an implied covenant of the existence of the way" (page 272). Applying these principles here we think that the judge erred in holding that deed under which the plaintiff claims gave her no easement over Wall Street as continued beyond the point where it joins her lot and that of the defendants. While the judge based his conclusion on the oral as well as the documentary evidence, we find nothing in the oral evidence which overcomes the effect of the deed on which the plaintiff's rights are based. To be sure, Wall Street along the plaintiff's westerly boundary had not been laid out at the time of the conveyance to Durkiwiez; nor was it shown on any plan referred to in his deed. But it was sufficiently designated by the reference in the deed so that the grantor and those claiming under him would be estopped to deny its existence, at least as far north as the plaintiff's westerly boundary extends. To that point the way could be ascertained with reasonable certainty. Moreover, a way to some extent was necessary to a reasonable enjoyment of the property conveyed, for the judge found that the plaintiff had a way not only by prescription by by necessity. A way created by estoppel, of course, "is not a way by necessity, and the right exists even if there be other ways either public or private leading to the land." New England Structural Co. v. Everett Distilling Co. 189 Mass. 145, 152. Hill v. Taylor, 296 Mass. 107, 116. We have considered the factor of necessity only as it may bear on the intent of the parties at the time of the conveyance to Durkiwiez. It is reasonable to infer, therefore, that the reference in the deed to the side line of Wall Street was intended to have its ordinary effect and would estop the grantor and those claiming under him from denying the existence of Wall Street along the plaintiff's westerly boundary.

The extent of the plaintiff's rights beyond the limits of her land "will depend upon, and may be shown by, extrinsic facts, as they existed at the time of the conveyance." Frawley v. Forrest, 310 Mass. 446, 451. Fox v. Union Sugar Refinery, 109 Mass. 292, 295-296. The question is one of fact. Driscoll v. Smith, 184 Mass. 221, 223. Since all of the evidence is before us, we are in a position to decide it. We are of opinion that the plaintiff's easement ought not to extend beyond the limits of her land. In the closely analogous situation involving the rights of grantees of lots bounded on a way shown on a plan referred to in a deed, the court in determining the extent of the easement has taken into consideration what was necessary for the enjoyment of the premises granted (although the necessity need not be an absolute or physical one) and whether the way referred to at its distant end connected directly or indirectly with a public highway. Wellwood v. Havrah Mishna Anshi Sphard Cemetery Corp. 254 Mass. 350, 355. See Prentiss v. Gloucester, 236 Mass. 36, 53. Here, if the extension of Wall Street were to be continued beyond the limits of the plaintiff's land, it would lead not directly or indirectly to any public way but only to the narrow strip along the river owned by the Commonwealth. It would not be necessary to any reasonable enjoyment of the granted premises. It is hardly conceivable that an extension of the way to that point was within the contemplation of the parties when the conveyance to Durkiwiez was make. Beyond the limits of the plaintiff's land it cannot be said that the way was "clearly indicated and prescribed." Frawley v. Forrest, 310 Mass. 446, 451.

It follows that the decree of the court below is reversed and a new decree is to be entered based on a right of way appurtenant to the plaintiff's land by the prolongation of Wall Street, at its original width, along the entire length of the plaintiff's western boundary. The plaintiff is to have costs of this appeal.

REFERENCES

Alfano, Paul J. *Creation and Termination of Highways in New Hampshire*. New Hampshire Bar Journal, March 1990: 33-40.

American Jurisprudence. Second Edition. Volume 12: *Boundaries*. Rochester: The Lawyers Cooperative Publishing Company. 1964.

American Jurisprudence. Second Edition. Volume 25: *Easements*. Rochester: The Lawyers Cooperative Publishing Company. 1964.

American Jurisprudence. Second Edition. Volume 26: *Eminent Domain* Rochester:The Lawyers Cooperative Publishing Company. 1964.

Backman, James H. and David A Thomas. 1989. A Practical Guide to Disputes Between Adjoining Landowners - Easements. New York: Matthew Bender & Company, Inc.

Black, Henry Campbell. 1944. *Black's Law Dictionary*. Third Edition. St. Paul:West Publishing Company. 1944 pp.

Corpus Juris Secundum. 1938. Volume 11: *Boundaries*. Brooklyn: The American Law Book Company.

Corpus Juris Secundum. 1938. Volume 28: *Easements*. Brooklyn: The American Law Book Company.

Creteau, Paul G. 1969. *Maine Real Estate Law*. Portland; Castle Publishing Company. 484 pp.

Hand, Jacqueline P. and James Charles Smith. 1988. *Neighboring Property Owners*. Colorado Springs: Shepard's McGraw-Hill, Inc. 462 pp.

Wattles, Gurdon H. 1976. *Writing Legal Descriptions*. Published by the author.

Wattles, William C. 1974. *Land Survey Descriptions*. Tenth Edition. Revised and Published by Gurdon H. Wattles. 140 pp.